Realism and

Logical Atomism

Realism and Logical Atomism

A Critique of Neo-Atomism from the Viewpoint of Classical Realism

John Peterson

Studies in the Humanities No. 14

Philosophy

The University of Alabama Press
University, Alabama

Library of Congress Cataloging in Publication Data:

Peterson, John, 1937–
    Realism and Logical Atomism: A Critique of Neo-
    Atomism from the Viewpoint of Classical Realism
    Includes Index.
    1. Logical atomism.   2. Realism.   3. Nominalism
I. Title.
BC199.L6P47   146'.5   75–12712
    ISBN 0–8173–6622–9

Contents

Realism and

Logical Atomism

Introduction

While this treatise is about logical atomism, it does not involve a detailed analysis of atomism as it appears in the thought of the two founders of logical atomism, Bertrand Russell and Ludwig Wittgenstein. Indeed, the logical atomism of the early Russell and early Wittgenstein has been so much discussed by philosophers and teachers of philosophy in the past few decades that another treatment of the same subject must surely travel over old roads. Consider, for example, the amount of material, both expository and critical, that has appeared in recent decades on Russell's logical atomism papers or on Wittgenstein's *Tractatus*. It is scarcely possible to think of another philosophical movement in recent Western philosophy about which there has been more intensive and more widespread commentary.

And yet, not everyone is aware that in the United States during the 60s' the philosophy of logical atomism took a decidedly ontological turn—a turn which was not only prompted by but which led to an increased preoccupation with the perennial realism-nominalism issue in philsoophy. I am speaking of the contemporary logical atomism of Professor Gustav

1

Bergmann and his school. If I understand Bergmann correctly, one of his aims as a philosopher is to offer a new defense of the metaphysics of logical atomism, a defense which rests ultimately not on a certain theory about propositions and the way they are related to facts, but on a certain view about the ontological status of properties. This latter view of Bergmann's is that properties or universals exist independently of minds. Bergmann's new defense of atomism, in other words, rests on Realism. But Realism is an ontological thesis, a thesis which answers in a certain way the fundamental philosophical question, "What sorts of things exist?" Moreover, it is Bergmann's view that the truth of philsoophical Realism is *itself* established not so much by logical or epistemological consideration as by the *real* facts of sameness and numerical difference among the things which are presented to us. Therefore, whether successfully or not, contemporary logical atomism is being defended ultimately on the basis of metaphysical rather than on logical grounds.

This does not mean to imply, however, and no logical atomist would hold, that Realism strictly implies logical atomism. For one could hold, as did the later Russell, for instance, that things are *nothing but* so many collections of universals. This is a form of Realism, but it is not logical atomism. For the latter holds not only that properties exist but that bare particulars or bare substances exist as well. Once more, one could hold, as did Plato, that there are both universals and particulars, but that the latter are neither simple nor as real as the former. But this again is not logical atomism though it is surely Realism. Still, whereas Realism is not a sufficient condition for logical atomism it is nonetheless a necessary condition for the same.[1] It follows from this that if Realism is once established then a first and most important step is taken in the direction of logical atomism.

Nevertheless, the latter-day logical atomists of whom we

have been speaking consider the remaining steps to logical atomism to be almost automatic. They take it as being obvious, for example, that universals must be exemplified by particulars. For if things were nothing but so many collections or bundles of universals as Russell held in his *An Inquiry into Meaning and Truth*, then it would be impossible to ground the numerical difference of two or more perfectly similar things. For if two things are composed of the very same properties, what makes them two and not one? Furthermore, since it just never occurs to contemporary atomists (as it seldom, if ever, occurs to most modern and recent philosophers) to construe universals as formal causes of particulars, as standards or archetypes which particulars approximate but always fall short of, these same latter-day logical atomists take it as axiomatic that particulars are as independent, self-enclosed and atom-like as are the universals which they exemplify. Moreover, if it came to defending the self-subsistent nature of the logical atomist's particular against the totally dependent nature of the Platonic particular, a philosopher like Bergmann would argue that if universals are the formal causes of particulars then they must be in some sense *constituents of* particulars. But in that case they would no longer be universals, for to be a constituent or part of something is to be particularized by and limited to that something. But universals *must* exist, according to Bergmann. Therefore, particulars are in no sense explained by universals in the sense that the latter are the formal causes of the former. Furthermore, a contemporary logical atomist would argue that on the basis of Platonic realism as on the basis of Russell's later Realism, no account of the numerical difference of two or more perfectly similar things is possible. For what would explain the numerical difference of two or more perfectly similar Platonic particulars? Hence, our atomist would hold that like the universals they exemplify, particulars must be complete, self-subsistent entities in their own right which are externally related to these universals in atom-like independence.

Nevertheless, whatever one may think of the rather facile way in which the contemporary atomist dismisses other forms of Realism than his own, still, it remains true that as a matter of historical fact the strength of logical atomism depends squarely on the strength of Realism. This means, of course, that if Realism is discredited then so also is logical atomism, though it does not work the other way around, as some atomists nowadays are prone to believe. In fact, not only are there forms of extreme Realism other than logical atomism, but also there are forms of Realism other than the extreme Realism of Plato, Russell or Gustav Bergmann. And yet, the paradox and, I think, the outstanding methodological weakness of the new logical atomism is that while it sets out on a program to transfer the defense of logical atomism from logical to ontological considerations, it simultaneously fails to recognize that other forms of Realism than logical atomism are as fully capable of explaining certain ontological data as is logical atomism. For example, as we shall argue in the chapters that follow, the moderate realism of a philosopher like Aquinas is as fully capable of grounding sameness and numerical difference as is the metaphysics of logical atomism. But if this is true, then it follows that the new, ontologically oriented defense of logical atomism is really not so indispensable as neo-atomists would have us believe. If contempoary logical atomists choose to transfer the rationale of atomism from logic to ontology, then they should in so doing be careful to show that the ontological data which they take to be explainable on the basis of logical atomism is explainable on that basis *alone*. Otherwise, there is really no point and no advantage to offering a new defense of logical atomism in the first place.

As a matter of fact, however, contemporary logical atomists do indeed hold that the sameness of two or more things can be grounded *only* by reifying properties or, in other words, only by construing properties as self-subsistent entities. And so they would argue that the moderate Realism of Aquinas, for example, simply falls short of accounting for sameness. But as we shall try to show in the later chapters which follow, given his belief that sameness must be ontologically grounded, the present-day logical atomist is forced to reify universals because he confuses a principle of a thing with a thing. Specifically, we shall find that because he falsely transfers to things attributes or features which belong only to what the Scholastics called principles of things, today's logical atomist can ground the sameness of two or more things *only* by reifying universals. But this reification of properties is unnecessary if only principles of things are not confused with things. Once having fallen into this confusion, therefore, it is not surprising that the contemporary logical atomist insists that the sameness of two or more things can be grounded only in terms of real self-subsistent universals, that is to say, only in terms of extreme Realism. For on the basis of that same confusion there simply is no other way to ground sameness.

And yet, as was said, this extreme Realism cannot, for our atomist, be Platonic in form. Otherwise, particulars would have to be construed as being causally dependent on properties for their very being, a view which, in the general framework of Platonism, would imply that particulars are complex entities composed of reflections or resemblances of properties. But then the question would arise, how could the numerical diversity of two or more of the Platonic particulars be grounded? The contemporary atomist would answer that the Platonist has nothing at all in his ontology with which to account for the numerical diversity of his complex particulars.

But even more than to their commitment to extreme Realism, critics of logical atomism have objected to the atomist's commitment to bare particulars. For it seems that when the logical atomist claims that there are certain entities which, taken in and of themselves, have no qualities or characteristics whatsoever (namely, bare particulars) he is clearly flying in the face of the central empiricist tenet that all knowledge of entities rests on experience. But who is, or ever could be, acquainted with a bare particular—something which has no sense qualities at all? Moreover, what particularly annoys these critics is that contemporary logical atomists like Gustav Bergmann claim to be adhering to the basic structure of empiricism. At one point, for example, Bergmann says that "the only primary reason I have to believe that something exists is that it is presented to me."[2] And he reconciles this claim with his commitment to bare particulars by holding that the latter, while not presented independently in sense perception, are nonetheless presented dependently in sense perception.

Understandably, critics of Bergmann construe this distinction between independent and dependent presentation as a kind of *deus ex machina* which Bergmann brings on the scene to remove the apparent contradiction between his advocacy of empiricism on the one hand and his commitment to bare particulars on the other. And so, these same critics would argue that Bergmann and the neo-atomists are not only wrong in abandoning empiricism but inconsistent in claiming to adhere to the strictures of empiricism while at the same time positing bare particulars.

And yet, this rather common objection to Bergmann's program, fatal though it may at first appear, may not really be unanswerable. For the objection is valid only if is assumed that Bergmann holds that objects which are presented *in* sense perception are also and necessarily recognized *by* sense perception. In classical British empiricism, of course, this is a safe assumption to make. If, therefore, the empiricism to which Bergmann claims to be faithful is the empiricism of Locke and Hume, then Bergmann's empiricism is indeed an inconsistent one in the light of his commitment to entities like bare particulars. But his commitment to these same entities is perfectly compatible with that older form of empiricism according to which objects which are presented *in* sense perception need not be recognized *by* sense perception. For it may well be the case that while entities like bare particulars are recognized only by the mind and never by sense perception, still they are nonetheless presented *in* sense perception. To paraphrase a metaphor Professor Gilson once used to explain the celebrated Scholastic maxim *"Nihil in intellectu quid non prius erat in sensu,"* "The senses carry a message which they cannot themselves interpret." Thus, if it is to the older, Scholastic form of empiricism that Bergmann swears allegiance, he could quite consistently uphold empiricism on the one hand while insisting on the existence of his bare particulars on the other. In other words, on the assumption of this type of empiricism he could compatibly say both that bare particulars exist and that a necessary condition for saying that anything exists is that it be presented in sense perception. For according to the Scholastic variety of empiricism all objects of knowledge are without exception presented *in* sense perception, though not all such objects are recognized *by* sense perception. Accordingly, when Bergmann says that his bare particulars are *in some sense* presented to us why cannot that sense be precisely the sense in which essences are presented to us according to Scholastic empiricism, i.e. present *in* sense perception but unrecognized *by* sense perception?

Nonetheless, critics of the new logical atomism would quickly and I think effectively reply that this would-be defense of Bergmann is really quite contrived. And this, not because the defense is in and of itself untenable, but because there is simply no evidence either that Bergmann himself ever draws the Scholastic distinction between being presented *in* sense perception and being recognized *by* sense perception or

that he acknowledges any other form of empiricism than the
classical British empiricism. In fact, our critic would doubt-
less point out that since the early Bergmann was a logical
positivist and logical positivism traces its origins to David
Hume, it follows that Bergmann himself falls in the tradition
of British empiricism. But if so, then it is reasonable to assume
that the empiricism to which Bergmann claims to be faithful
is no other than classical British empiricism. And if this is the
case, then it is of no use to try to reconcile Bergmann's professed empiricism with his commitment to bare particulars by
identifying Bergmann's empiricism with Scholastic instead of
with British empiricism.

It appears certain, then, that the logical atomist must either
abandon bare particulars or else abandon empiricism. But since
to abandon bare particulars is tantamount to giving up logical
atomism, it follows that any logical atomist, be he Russell,
Wittgenstein, or Bergmann, must either surrender his atomism
or else renounce empiricism. Recognizing this ultimate incompatibility between logical atomism and empiricism, Bertrand
Russell chose to abandon logical atomism. But principally because they view logical atomism as an ontology on the basis
of which *alone* sameness and numerical diversity can be
grounded, neo-atomists like Bergmann have chosen, at least
implicitly, to surrender empiricism instead. And yet, as was
mentioned earlier, sameness and numerical diversity can be
grounded without positing such entities as bare particulars
and without reifying properties, if what merely belongs to
things is not falsely assimilated to principles of things. And
so, since logical atomism is not necessary for explaining sameness and numerical difference to begin with, it follows that,
contrary to what the neo-atomist believes, the possibility of
grounding sameness and numerical difference is not a good or
sufficient reason for choosing logical atomism over empiricism.

Finally, we must here just indicate what we shall later

explain in more detail, namely, how or in what respect the logical atomist confuses a principle of a thing with a thing, and how that confusion leads him directly to extreme Realism.

Briefly, the atomist begins by insisting that the similarity of two things must be grounded in properties or universals. Two green spots are similar by virtue of the property of greenness, and two round spots are similar by virtue of the property of roundness, etc. Universals or properties, therefore, must exist as the ontological ground of similarity. But universals or properties are by definition one. There may be many green spots, for example, but there is only one greenness. Hence, two or more green spots do not *contain* the property greenness; otherwise, greenness would be numerically many which by definition it cannot be. Rather, these same spots each and every one of them stand in a certain external relation to the property of greenness. This means that taken in and of themselves these spots are characterless (bare) particulars.

The questionable assumption here is that universals or properties are by definition numerically one. To assume that they are, we shall find, is to transfer to a principle or constituent of a thing an attribute or feature which belongs only to a thing. And it is on this false assimilation of principles of things to things that the philosophy of logical atomism rests.

I. Logical Atomism Revisited: A New Departure

1. THE OLDER AND NEWER METHODOLOGY OF LOGICAL ATOMISTS

As a contemporary American philosopher observed some few years ago, "realism and nominalism may well be perennial issues in philosophy."[1] And perhaps the strongest reason for the recurrence of these issues lies in the fact that, while they are in themselves ontological positions, realism and nominalism alike are frequently the logical consequence or outcome of points of view taken in other areas of Philosophy than metaphysics, especially in theory of knowledge and in logic. It is not just by accident, for instance, that most of the great British philosophers of the past two centuries, thoroughgoing empiricists as regards epistemology, were committed straightaway to a nominalistic ontology. Moreover, that this same sort of indirect adoption of realism or nominalism is particularly the case in our own century is readily witnessed in the dispute between some realist philosophers like Russell and Wittgenstein on the one hand, and nominalist thinkers like W. V. Quine on the other. Russell's logical atomism, for instance, is the direct result of both his picture theory of propositions and his Theory of Descriptions.[2] By the same token, Quine's rejection of logical atomism and his adherence to a "fact ontology" instead stem from nothing other than his empiricist theory of knowledge. Once again and on the contemporary scene, the current prolonged debate among logical theorists as to whether Wittgenstein's *Tractatus* is nominalistic or realistic not only indicates the seriousness with which the realism-nominalism issue is generally taken by the disputants in question but also gives ample testimony, through one of the arguments in that dispute, to the thesis just expressed. More specifically, the leading exponent for a nominalist interpretation of the *Tractatus*, G. E. M. Anscombe, argues that Wittgenstein's *objects* preclude properties or universals on the basis of the logical consideration that according to Wittgenstein's picture theory atomic sentences do not contain any function signs.[3]

Nevertheless, despite the tendency among contemporary analytic philosophers to derive ontology from logic or epistemology—to decide what sorts of things exist on the basis of their own logical or epistemological theories—we find among contemporary logical atomists like Gustav Bergmann an unmistakable reversal of method in this regard. That is to say, we find a tendency on the part of contemporary atomists to ground or justify both the metaphysics of logical atomism and the picture theory which historically gave rise to it, strictly on the basis of ontology or metaphysics itself. Thus, instead of taking the form of a kind of deduction from certain logical theories about the relation of propositions to facts, the metaphysics of logical atomism is justified or grounded by contemporary atomists largely in terms of its ability to ground sameness and numerical difference. And once justified on this ontological basis, this same metaphysics of logical atomism is then used by the neo-atomists to justify the picture theory of propositions. In other words, it appears that contemporary logical atomists have adopted an entirely new defense of their philosophical program. What was once the condition of logical atomism, the picture theory of propositions, has now become conditioned by logical atomism. Originally deduced from certain logical considerations about the nature of propositions, the metaphysics of logical atomism in its most recent form is put forward as an answer to certain perennial ontological difficulties. Thus in their own way and to the extent that they have subordinated logical theory to metaphysics, contemporary logical atomists have resurrected and reasserted the medieval notion of metaphysics as being "first philosophy."

That the earlier atomism of Russell and Wittgenstein issued from logical rather than from ontological considerations goes almost without saying. Indeed, this is the reason why it is called *logical* atomism. Having adopted Frege's view that every proposition can be divided into a function-sign and an argument-sign, Bertrand Russell for instance went on to argue that the complexity of the proposition mirrored or mapped a corresponding complexity in reality. At one point he remarks:

> . . . in a logically correct symbolism there will always be a certain fundamental identity of structure between a fact and the symbol for it; and that the complexity of the symbol corresponds very closely with the complexity of the fact symbolized by it. Also, as I said before, it is quite directly evident to inspection that the fact, for example, that two things stand in a certain relation to one another—e.g., that this is to the left of that—is itself objectively complex, and not merely that the apprehension of it is complex. The fact that two things stand in a certain relation to each other, or any statement of that sort, has a complexity all of its own. I shall therefore in future assume that there is an objective complexity in the world, and that it is mirrored by the complexity of propositions.[4]

It was Russell's view, then, that the key to knowing what kinds of ultimate entities there are in the world is to be found in the analysis of propositions. If we take the simplest type of proposition, then, say, "This is red," we shall have to conclude

that corresponding to the simple argument-sign "This" there
is a simple, bare particular,[5] and that corresponding to the
simple function-sign "red" there is a simple function or universal. In other words, at this early stage of his philosophical
odyssey Russell held that to the difference between names and
predicates on the level of the logical or the linguistic, corres-
ponded a difference between the entities signified by these
symbols on the level of the real. But unlike Frege, Russell
denied that the entities signified by function terms or predicates were ontologically incomplete or dependent entities.[6]

2. REASONS FOR THE ONTOLOGICAL TURN IN
CONTEMPORARY LOGICAL ATOMISM

And yet, in view of this original logical grounding of the
metaphysics of logical atomism and considering the present-
day subordination of metaphysics to logic, one would naturally be curious as to just what brought about the methodological
reversal among contemporary atomists of which we are
speaking. Why, in other words, do the neo-logical atomists
now choose to give their atomism an ontological rather than a
logical foundation?

In answer, we find that present-day atomists began to realize
that since the denial of the identification of meaning and
referent in a name on the part of some logicians posed a serious
threat to the picture theory of propositions, it would become
increasingly difficult to use the picture theory of propositions
as a ground for the metaphysics of logical atomism. For if
meaning and referent are distinct even in singular terms that
are genuine names for objects, then the old argument against
propositions being *names* (and not pictures) for facts simply
goes by the board. Briefly stated, that argument is as follows:
If meaning and referent are identical in a name, then if propositions are names for facts, then either false propositions name

"false facts," or else the meaning of a proposition is different depending on whether the proposition is true or false. But each part of the latter disjunct is absurd. Hence, propositions can be construed as being names for facts only if it is denied that a name's meaning is identical with its referent. Instead of being viewed as pictures of facts, therefore, propositions (at least true ones) could (if meaning is distinguished from referent in a name) just as well be taken as names for facts; for so long as names are construed in such a way that their meaning and referent are distinct, false propositions, instead of naming such inadmissable entities as "false facts," would simply have no referent at all, even though they would be quite meaningful.

In other words, the point is that no sooner is the picture theory rendered arbitrary as a result of distinguishing meaning from referent in a name, than the metaphysics of logical atomism is deprived of its main support; for in the logical atomism of Russell and Wittgenstein it was precisely from the picture theory of propositions that the metaphysics of logical atomism was deduced.

Faced then with this serious challenge to the necessity of the picture theory and the atomistic metaphysics that stemmed from it, contemporary atomists clearly had two lines of defense: either they had to show conclusively that the logic of names somehow inherently forbade any distinction between the meaning and referent of a name, or else they had to construct a defense of the metaphysics of logical atomism and indirectly a defense of the picture theory on other than purely logical grounds. And in view of their constant reiteration that it is only through such simple entities as bare particulars and universals that the ontological problem of accounting for sameness and numerical difference, for example, can be resolved, it is clear that latter-day atomists have chosen the second line of defense.

But even if the opponents of logical atomism are correct about the distinction between meaning and referent in a name, that distinction is not the *raison d'etre* of their dismissal of the picture theory. It merely serves to make possible what would otherwise be absurd, namely, the alternate theory that true propositions are names for facts. Rather, their refusal to give the picture theory a hearing is the direct result of their outright rejection of the ontology of logical atomism with its firm commitment to such occult entities as bare particulars and properties. One of these opponents of atomism, W. V. Quine, holds that only that which is or can be an object of acquaintance can be named and therefore be said to exist. But Quine and others would insist that since neither bare particulars nor properties are ever presented in sense perception, they can never be either one of them legitimate objects of acquaintance. It has often been pointed out that Quine is a nominalist. While this is certainly true, it would be more illuminating to say that his nominalism is the result of a deeply-rooted empiricism.

But if logical atomism is unacceptable because it violates what has sometimes been called the Principle of Acquaintance[7] then so too, Quine would argue, is the picture theory of propositions, for the latter leads directly to the former. To explain, according to the very meaning of the picture theory, the S-term of a simple subject-predicate proposition must name a bare particular, an entity without any descriptive properties whatsoever; otherwise, it would not be a genuine subject-predicate proposition, but an existential one instead. For according to Russell's Theory of Descriptions, all descriptive elements are to be relegated to the function or predicate side of a proposition, leaving nothing in the subject-place of a subject-predicate proposition but logically proper names as opposed, say, to ordinary or grammatical names which, strictly speaking, are not names at all. But logically proper names can only name bare particulars. It follows, therefore, that to dismiss the metaphysics of logical atomism (and hence to dismiss bare particulars) is, if one adheres strictly to the Theory of Descriptions, simultaneously to eliminate subject-predicate or elementary propositions.[8] But since it is precisely subject-predicate or elementary propositions which are said to be logical pictures of facts according to the picture theory, it follows that to abandon logical atomism is also to abandon the picture theory of propositions. But clinging to Russell's Theory of Descriptions, and unwilling to admit such occult entities as bare particulars and properties, a philosopher like Quine has no other choice than to reject the picture theory of propositions altogether.

Now, in light of this empirically-motivated criticism of logical atomism and the picture theory, contemporary atomists apparently decided to make their defense of logical atomism and hence the picture theory turn on the ontological point of accounting for sameness and numerical difference. In other words and more specifically, how, our atomist would inquire, can the numerical diversity of two or more exactly similar things be explained or ontologically grounded without recourse to bare particulars? Further, in the absence of real properties or universals, how, he would again ask, can the exact sameness of these same things be metaphysically accounted for? Thus, as a rejoinder to the ultra-empiricist criticism of Quine and other opponents of logical atomism, contemporary logical atomists shift their point of view from a logical one in which the metaphysics of logical atomism is viewed more or less as a consequence of the picture theory, to an ontological one in which that same metaphysics is put forth as an ontology in terms of which alone sameness and difference can be explained.

And yet, it was not, to repeat, because of its supposed ability to account for sameness and numerical difference that logical atomism was originally adopted. When Russell in his logical

atomism papers and Wittgenstein in the *Tractatus* construct
an atomistic metaphysics they each of them do so out of purely
logical considerations. It is no secret, for instance, that taking
over entirely the argument-function analysis of propositions
originally conceived by Gottlob Frege, Bertrand Russell simply announced that there must be in reality certain atomic
entities corresponding to the argument and function signs
respectively in the propositions. And the more complex the
symbolism was in terms of there being more than one argument-sign for the same function-sign, the more complex the
corresponding fact had to be that was being pictured or mirrored by the whole symbol.

Nor is Wittgenstein's point of departure in the *Tractatus*
based on anything other than logical considerations. While it
is true that the opening pages of that enigmatic treatise are
devoted exclusively to what the world is made up of, it is
clear that this early discussion about objects and facts is sub-
ordinate to and consequent upon the main logical issue with
which Wittgenstein is concerned in the *Tractatus*, namely,
the question of what kind of relation a sentential fact must
bear to another fact in order that the former can be a symbol
for the latter. Moreover, it is common knowledge that for the
early Wittgenstein the fact that the meaningfulness of a proposition does not depend on other propositions being true presupposes atomism or the view that the world is composed of
ultimate simples.[9] Thus, the ground of atomism for the early
Wittgenstein is logical and epistemological and not ontological
or metaphysical.

And yet, though we shall argue in later chapters that contemporary logical atomists ultimately contradict themselves
in attempting to explain sameness and numerical difference in
the way they do while still clinging to metaphysical atomism,
it is nonetheless to their credit that they recognize the necessity of constructing a theory of propositions that will allow

for a solution to this ontological problem. In fact, it is precisely on this basis that they defend the picture theory's analysis of the "is" relation of simple atomic sentences as over against either the whole-part or identity analyses which, they argue, end up precluding an explanation of either exact sameness or numerical difference.[10] This pointedly illustrates their fully warranted concern to gear logical theory to the requirements of ontology.

On the other hand, however, and in contrast, one of the chief contemporary opponents of logical atomism, W. V. Quine, apparently regards any attempt at grounding sameness and numerical diversity in simple atomic entities of various kinds as entirely unnecessary and fruitless. For Quine, facts are "ultimate and reducible," for any attempt to analyse them further only leads to strange, occult entities which by the principles of empiricism are entirely inadmissable. As Quine himself puts it:

> One may admit that there are red houses, roses, and sunsets, but deny, except as a popular and misleading manner of speaking, that they have anything in common. The words 'houses,' 'roses,' and 'sunsets' are true of sundry individual entities which are houses and roses and sunsets, and the word 'red' or 'red object' is true of each of sundry individual entities which are red houses, red roses, red sunsets; but there is not, in addition, any entity whatever, individual or otherwise, which is named by the word 'redness,' nor, for that matter, by word 'household,' 'rosehood,' 'sunsethood.' That the houses and roses and sunsets are all of them red may be taken as ultimate and irreducible, and it may be held that McX is not better off, in point of real explanatory power, for all the occult entities which he posits under such names as 'redness.'[11]

Quine's basic empiricism, of course, provides the background for this comment. Instead of analysing out of facts

certain strange entities that will supposedly explain both their
exact similarity to, but numerical difference from, other facts,
why not, Quine would ask, take these same facts as "ultimate
and irreducible"? After all, we are all of us directly acquainted
with facts—with the fact for instance, that a house is red. But
how can we honestly claim to be acquainted with *house-ness*,
redness, or a certain bare particular exemplifying either one or
both of these abstract entities?

3. THE POSSIBILITY OF SYNTHESIS OF THE EXTREMES OF REALISM AND NOMINALISM

Nevertheless, while one can certainly understand and even
share Quine's reservations about counting bare particulars and
universals as really existent things, still, one cannot help but
detect a certain arbitrariness in Quine's abrupt characterization
of facts as "ultimate and irreducible." After all, is it not both
meaningful and necessary to seek the principle in virtue of
which "red houses, red roses and red sunsets" are all of them
placed in the same class of red things? And if we are presented
with two exactly similar green discs, is it not again quite meaningful and necessary to seek the principle of their numerical
diversity? Nor does it necessarily follow that any answer to
these questions must automatically be in terms of bare particulars and real universals. And finally, why must entities be
called occult or strange just because they fail to be the sort of
things that can be recognized by sense perception? For is it
not possible that some entities can be present *in* sense perception without necessarily being recognized *by* sense perception?

With this we are brought at last to the more constructive
side of our argument. This will consist mainly in an attempt
to show how, on the basis of the traditional Thomistic theory
of essences, a theory of propositions can be constructed that
will not only allow for an explanation of both the sameness

and numerical difference of two or more facts *without* recourse to such strange entities as bare particulars and real
universals, but that will also allow us human knowers to be
able to know and to say *what* something or other is, an advantage that is not shared by the picture theory of propositions.
Thus, we shall argue that on the basis of the Thomistic theory
of essences it is possible to combine the best features of each
of the opposed positions we have here been discussing. Concretely, while avoiding, as does a contemporary nominalist like
Quine, a commitment to any such things as bare particulars or
real universals, Aquinas can still, like the neo-atomists, provide
a ground for sameness and numerical difference, something
which no nominalist can do.

In his early treatise *De Ente et Essentia* St. Thomas Aquinas
clearly shows how a solution to the logical problem of predication is possible only on the basis of a metaphysical theory of
essences.[12] Stated less technically, what this comes down to is
that in order for us human knowers to assert *what* anything is
in and through propositions, it is necessary for us to presuppose
beings or more precisely principles of being that in Scholastic
terminology are known as absolute essences. And yet, while
predication is possible according to Aquinas only on the presupposition of these essences, still, it does not follow from this
that St. Thomas simply deduced his metaphysics from his
theory of predication. In other words, Aquinas did not establish his metaphysics by asking the question, in Kantian fashion,
"granted that we can make "what-statements," how is it possible"? Rather, he is already convinced of the necessity of the
doctrine of essences on strictly metaphysical grounds, namely,
on the grounds that essences are required in order to account
for real similarity among individuals. But it is nonetheless true
that his doctrine of essence fulfills a dual function: it both
allows for and explains real similarity among things (its onto-

logical function) and allows us to predicate one thing of another (its logical function).

Be that as it may, however, we must now directly turn our attention to the new defense of the metaphysics of logical atomism in order to understand how contemporary logical atomists propose to justify the existence of bare particulars and properties, and, in so doing, build an ontological foundation for the picture theory of atomic propositions.

II. Existence Criteria
and the Issues of
Realism and Nominalism

1. SAMENESS, DIFFERENCE AND THE
'IS'-RELATION IN SUBJECT-PREDICATE STATEMENTS

Contemporary logical atomists often distinguish two criteria for existence or two "ontological criteria." The first criterion, which they associate with what they consider the nominalist point of view, states that what exists is independent. The second citerion, which they themselves adopt and which they associate with Realism, asserts that only what is named exists. Not surprisingly, they call the former criterion the *independence criterion*, whereas they label the latter criterion the *naming criterion*.[1]

In this chapter I should like first to explore and elucidate the important philosophical background of each of these criteria, especially that of the naming criterion, indicating the kinds of logical, epistemological or ontological considerations which have led more or less directly to the adoption of each one of them. More specifically, I will show how, by a strict and characteristic adherence to what is commonly called the Principle of Acquaintance, contemporary Nominalists like W. V. Quine must embrace the independence criterion while, on the other hand and largely as a result of their concern to provide an ontological account of sameness and numerical diversity, logical atomists like Gustav Bergmann are forced to adopt the naming criterion.

More specifically and with respect to this central issue of explaining sameness and numerical difference, a leading contemporary atomist, E. B. Allaire has warned of the serious ontological consequences that ensue once the logical atomist's analysis of simple atomic propositions is abandoned—once, in other words, the terms 'This' and 'red' in the atomic sentence "This is red," for example, are no longer interpreted as naming a bare particular and a universal respectively.[2] Concretely and according to Allaire, if bare particulars were abandoned in such a way that the subject term 'This' in "This is red," referred not to a *bare particular* but rather to a *collection of universals* of which what is signified by the predicate term 'red' were a *part*, then there would be nothing to account for the numerical diversity of, say, *two* perfectly similar red discs. On the other hand, Allaire continues, if universals are abandoned in such a way that the subject term 'This' in the same sentence referred to a *collection of "perfect particulars"*[3] of which what is signified by the predicate term 'red' were a part, then in that case there would be nothing to account for the sameness of these two discs.

Now if these two part-whole analyses were the only alternative ways of interpreting the sentence "This is red," then Allaire's atomistic account of simple atomic propositions would be unassailable. In other words, as it stands, his argument is directed only against two extreme ontological alternatives: 1) The ultra-Realistic position that only universals exist and 2) The Nominalistic position that only perfect particulars exist.

Contemporary atomists who reject the part-whole analysis of simple atomic propositions also reject the alternative that the copula 'is' expresses identity in such propositions, and once again for ontological reasons. If, they argue, the copula in the sentence "This is red" expresses identity then it must also express identity in the sentence "That is red." But from this it follows that "This is that." Hence, the thesis that the copula in simple atomic propositions expresses an identity relation fails to account for the numerical diversity of the two similar things.[4]

As against this double denial, we shall later argue for the very opposite position, namely, that any so-called atomic proposition, while it signifies or intends a real whole-part relation, is at the same time, in itself a relation of identity. We shall there contend that on such a view of propositions and on the assumption that there are such things as natures or essences, an ontological explanation of sameness and numerical diversity can be achieved without admitting as real entities such occult entities as bare particulars and universals. Moreover, we shall contend that on the basis of such an analysis of predication one is able to account for the fact that we are able to know and to say just *what* some particular thing or other really is—an epistemological feat which the atomists' analysis of simple atomic propositions precludes.

2. THE NAMING CRITERION AND THE INDEPENDENCE CRITERION COMPARED

But to return to the topic at hand, namely, an analysis of the naming and independence criteria for existence, let us state what each of these criteria claims and then show why our atomist adopts the naming criterion and rejects the independence criterion.

According to the independence criterion facts exist whereas properties do not. This gives us a clue as to the interpretation of 'independent' in this context. Atomic facts are independent of each other[5] in a way that bare particulars and properties are not independent of each other. For neither bare particulars nor properties are *found by themselves*, as it were. In neo-atomist terminology, every particular exemplifies at least one property, and every property is exemplified by at least one particular.[6] In this sense properties and bare particulars are dependent, while facts are independent.[7] Moreover, those who adhere to what atomists call the independence criterion do so because of a prior commitment to three other assertions: (a) that what exists can be named and *vice versa*, (b) that what is named must be the sort of thing that can be presented in sense perception, and (c) that if anything be the sort of thing that can be presented in sense perception, then if it is named, it exists independently. From these three assertions, it follows (d) that what exists is independent.

Ultimately, however, the ground for this independence criterion is epistemological in nature in the sense that its adoption is conditioned by the assumption, implicit in (c) above, that there is a kind of one-to-one correspondence between the way in which objects are presented in sense perception and the way in which such objects exist, if in fact they do exist. If, in other words, an object of acquaintance actually exists, then the way in which it exists will correspond to the way in which it is presented in sense perception. But since every object of acquaintance is presented independently, so too the object to which it corresponds in reality (if in fact there be such an object), exists independently. Stated differently, since we are acquainted with something-that-is-red rather than with redness itself, then what exists, if anything, is the former and not the latter. But as an object of acquaintance the former is independent in a sense in which the latter is not. We are acquainted with "a red something" independently of being acquainted with anything else. But we are acquainted with *red* only dependently, i.e., only by dint of being acquainted with "a red something." This describes the pattern of reasoning which neo-atomists ascribe to contemporary "fact ontologists," i.e., those who hold that complex *facts* and not simple things are the ultimate constituents of the world.[8]

Adhering to (a) above, namely, that what is named exists, and holding (1) that what is named is somehow presented in sense perception, (2) that what is named is simple, and (3) that what is simple is dependent in the sense described, our atomist must, of course, reject (c) above, namely, that if anything is presented in sense perception then, if it exists, it must be independent. Moreover in accepting the three immediately previous assertions, our latter-day atomist must simultaneously broaden the scope of objects which are, or can be, objects of acquaintance. In effect, he must hold that we are presented in sense perception not only with independent, complex entities, but also with dependent, simple entities; that we are, in other words, somehow presented with bare particulars and characters as well as with facts. The claim that we are acquainted with characters as well as with facts might conceivably be supported by making a distinction between objects that are presented independently (facts) and objects that are presented perhaps, dependently (characters). But the claim that we are in any sense presented with bare particulars is immeasurably more difficult to support. In fact, the major point of criticism that is nowadays directed against contemporary atomism seems to center on the point that, in positing bare particulars as well as properties as existents, atomists have openly violated the Principle of Acquaintance, perhaps the cardinal tenet of empiricism.[9]

But aside from this common criticism and even granting for the moment that our atomist's commitment to bare particulars is not incompatible with his acceptance of (b) above, what is it, basically, that distinguishes the naming criterion from the independence criterion? The difference, obvious as it may appear, must still be spelled out, since the recognition of that difference is the first step in revealing the thoroughly ontological orientation of contemporary atomism—an orientation that takes the form of a genuine and fully justifiable concern on the part of many atomists for finding a solution to the Realism-Nominalism issue.

Briefly stated, built into the *naming criterion* is the notion that what is named is simple, while conversely, imbedded in the independence criterion is the idea that what is named is complex. Thus, the fundamental difference between the two criteria in question is rooted in a difference in the objects named in each case. That what is named (and hence that what exists) is complex follows from the two premises that what is named is independent and that what is independent is complex. The first premise follows from (a), (b) and (c) above, while the second premise follows from (b) above together with the assertion that what is presented in sense perception is complex, i.e., that we are acquainted with things-that-are-red rather than with redness itself.

On the other hand, the ground for the atomists' assertion that what is named (and hence, again, that what exists) is simple is not empirical or epistemological, but ultimately onto-logical in nature. To be sure, latter-day atomists inherit and defend Russell's analysis of simple atomic propositions, ac-cording to which (such propositions being "maps" or "pic-tures" of simple atomic facts) the subject and predicate terms name simple entities, i.e., particulars and universals respec-tively. Nevertheless, as we have seen from Allaire's argument, for instance, such an analysis of simple atomic propositions is itself grounded in and supported by a prevailing ontological attempt to solve, by means of positing such simple entities as bare particular and universals, the problem of sameness and numerical difference as it occurs on the level of complex enti-ties or facts. Yet, as has been pointed out, by introducing such simple entities as bare particulars as existents, our contempo-rary atomist also and simultaneously runs the risk of violating the Principle of Acquaintance.[10]

Still, even if the atomist does violate this Principle, that is to say, even if there is no way in which we can be said to be acquainted with bare particulars, it is not on the basis of this that we shall criticize contemporary logical atomism. Rather, our criticism will take the form of a critique of the ontology which has given rise to this alleged violation and which, because it supposedly accounts for sameness and numerical difference, might for that reason and in some quarters be judged indispensable despite any such violation. Concretely, we shall criticize this ontology not so much for failing to account for sameness and diversity on the level of facts but for engendering the *same* sameness-diversity problem on the level of simples where it can be solved by our atomist only by his conceding that these simples are not really simple after all. In other words, our argument will be that the way in which a contemporary logical atomist explains sameness and numerical diversity is ultimately incompatible with his professed atomism.

3. THE STRENGTH OF THE ATOMISTS' CRITIQUE OF CONTEMPORARY NOMINALISM

Nevertheless, as regards grounding sameness and numerical difference on the level of facts and as against those who hold to the independence criterion (whom the neo-atomists call Nominalists), our atomist or Realist to all appearances at least presents a plausible case. For if, on the one hand, the copula 'is' in, say, "This is red" expresses a relation of identity, (in which case both 'This' and 'red' would name the same complex thing-that-is-red), then our Nominalist could provide no explanation for the numerical diversity of say, two red things. Moreover, on the other hand, if the copula in this same sentence expresses a whole-part relation in such a way that "This is red" would be interpreted as meaning "red is a part of this," then, as Allaire is quick to point out, depending on whether

the predicate 'red' signifies a "perfect particular" or a universal, no account could be given of either the sameness or the
numerical difference of two perfectly similar red things.

Finally, and according to the neo-atomist, a second analysis
of the whole-part interpretation of simple atomic propositions,
one which would render "This is red" and "This is a part of
red," can be adopted by the nominalist only at the price of
being inconsistent or arbitrary. For on this interpretation of
"This is red," the predicate 'red' signifies a whole composed
of all the red things in the world. But unless he chooses to
abandon the independence criterion the nominalist cannot
affirm the existence of this "whole," for such a "whole" is not
and could not be presented in sense perception.[11] Not only
that, but the introduction of this real whole would conflict
with the basic nominalist thesis that only individuals exist, for
instead of having just individuals as existents our nominalist
would be forced to admit another kind of entity, i.e., groups
of individuals. And then according to the atomist, he would
be at a loss to explain what there was in or about a certain
particular thing which caused it to belong to one class of
individuals rather than to another.

On the other hand, however, should the nominalist retort
by insisting that he never intended such a whole to be taken
as a real thing in the first place but only as a mental entity,
then though he has now not violated the independence criterion, he is still forced to explain what there is in or about a
certain individual which causes us in coming to know that
thing to place it in the same class with other individuals. Moreover, by interpreting "This is red" as "This is a member of the
class of red things" where the class of red things is taken as an
ens rationis, we are surely presupposing that what is referred
to by the subject 'This' is really and in fact red! Otherwise,
it would be senseless to say that, logically speaking, it belongs
to the class of red things. By the same token, the sentence

"That is red" interpreted as "That is a member of the class of red things" would presuppose that what is referred to by the subject term 'That' is also in fact red. In other words, any attempt to say what 'This' or 'That' is logically speaking, that is to say, any attempt to ascribe that property which 'This' or 'That' acquires as a result of *being known* namely, the property of being a member of a certain class (say the class of red things), presupposes that the thing referred to has as one of its constituents *in rerum natura* the property red. But this is to say that in the real as opposed to the logical order, the referent of 'This' or 'That' is an existent whole of which any property signified by the predicate (say red) is a subsistent part. But precisely at this point a contemporary atomist would present to the Nominalist the kind of ontological dilemma with respect to providing an account of sameness and numerical difference which Allaire, for one, refers to and which was discussed above.

In sum, our atomist rejects both the identity and the whole-part analyses of simple atomic propositions. The identity analysis, he argues, fails to account for the numerical diversity of similar things. The *first version* of the whole-part analysis he says, fails to account for either the sameness or the numerical difference of two or more perfectly similar things, depending on whether the predicate refers to a perfect particular or a universal. Finally, according to the neo-atomist, the first interpretation of the *second version* of the whole-part analysis, involving as it does the reification of classes, is inconsistent with the nominalistic independence criterion while the second interpretation of this second version of the whole-part analysis brings us back to the same ontological dilemma to which the first version of that analysis gives rise. Accordingly, contemporary atomists reject both the identity and whole-part analyses of simple atomic propositions and adopt instead the atomistic thesis that the subject and predicate terms of such propo-

sitions name different kinds of simple entities (bare particulars
and universals respectively) which enter into a relationship of
"exemplification." Only this analysis, they hold, can account
for sameness and numerical diversity on the level of complex
entities or facts.[12]

4. THE STATUS OF THE EXEMPLIFICATION-TIE—A PROBLEM FOR THE ATOMISTS

And yet, in attempting to cope with the ontological problem
of sameness and numerical difference by resorting to such
entities as bare particulars and universals, contemporary atomists not only run the risk of violating a principle which they
themselves supposedly espouse (i.e. the Principle of Acquaintance), but they have also been forced to explain just what
kind of relation the copula 'is' expresses in simple atomic propositions if it expresses neither an identity nor a whole-part
relation. To be sure, contemporary atomists do have a name
for the relation, or better, the nexus, that obtains between a
bare particular and a universal, namely, the *exemplification-tie*,
but as to just how this nexus or tie is to be understood is not
immediately clear. When, in ordinary English we say that
something or other *exemplifies* a certain property we mean
to say that the particular thing in question actually and in fact
has that property. But this ordinary meaning of the phrase
'x exemplifies y' cannot be what our atomist appeals to when
he says that a bare particular exemplifies a property or universal, for any and every bare particular just as such is utterly
characterless, which is to say that in and of itself it *has* no
properties at all.

But then, what extra-ordinary or philosophical meaning do
the atomists of today attach to the term 'exemplification,' or,
what comes to the same thing, what do they mean when they
say that a bare particular *exemplifies* a property? Apparently,
the phrase in its technical sense means that one kind of simple

existent (a bare particular) is extrinsically or externally tied to another kind of simple existent (a universal; that these two kinds of existents, though they stand against each other in atom-like independence, are related to each other as part to part to form a complex entity (an atomic fact).

And yet, while this exemplification-tie is in some sense an extrinsic or external one, still, it cannot be on a par with such ordinary external relations as "to the left of," "above," "to be north of," etc., for unlike these latter relations, the exemplification-tie does not exist but only subsists. In fact, it is precisely *because* it is not a thing that the atomists deny that the exemplification-tie is strictly speaking a relation, since relations, being kinds of universals, are things according to the atomist. One reason for our atomist's denial, as we shall discover, is connected with the famous Bradleian paradox as regards relations. But another reason for his denial of thinghood to the exemplification-tie, one which we shall now examine, is connected with the Realism-Nominalism issue, or more concretely, with our atomist's constant and fully warranted concern with solving the problem of sameness and numerical difference.

As regards this second reason, we should observe that just as it was out of a concern to explain sameness and numerical difference on the level of complex things or facts that led our atomist (a) to introduce bare particulars and universals as things and therefore (b) to posit the exemplification-tie as opposed to either the whole-part-"is" or the identity-"is," so too, it is at least partially out of this same concern on another level that leads him to deny thinghood to the exemplification-tie. Specifically, were this nexus a thing, then since the only kinds of things acknowledged by the atomists are bare particulars and universals, the exemplification-tie would have to be either particular or universal. But neither alternative is possible if either the sameness or the numerical difference of

two or more exemplification-ties is to be accounted for. To
explain, if the nexus were in itself particular, then it would be
impossible to account for the sameness, say, of the two ties
expressed by the copula 'is' in the atomic sentences "This is
red" and "That is red" respectively. Second, if the nexus were
in itself universal, then it would be equally impossible to
account for the numerical diversity of the same two ties.
Hence, our atomist must conclude that, being neither particular nor universal in itself, the exemplification-tie is not a
thing or does not "exist."[13]

5. SIMILARITY OF THIS ARGUMENT TO THAT OF AQUINAS

Now this pattern of accounting for sameness while allowing
for numerical difference is not new. In fact, as shall be shown
in a later chapter, St. Thomas Aquinas resorts to a similar
pattern of explanation in and through his theory of essences.
Being neither particular nor universal in itself, an essence can
simultaneously account for sameness and allow for numerical
diversity. Moreover, we shall also have occasion to show what
at this point we can merely suggest: that not only is the atomist's exemplification-tie identifiable with a Thomistic essence,
but also that his "properties" of individuality and universality
(which are constituents of bare particulars and universals
respectively) are identifiable with what St. Thomas took to be
an essence. Further, we shall find that the atomist's attempt,
by means of positing bare particulars and universals, to explain
sameness and numerical difference on the level of facts only
serves to recreate the same problems of sameness and numerical difference on the level of particulars and universals themselves. But on this level, only an appeal to essences in the guise
of "properties" can solve the problem in question. Accordingly, we shall argue that, having discarded essences or
natures as a possible solution to the problem of the One and
the Many on the level of facts (resorting to bare particulars

and universals instead), our latter-day atomist then goes on to re-introduce what amount to essences on the level of simples in order to resolve the same problem on that level. But once having introduced these "disguised essences," our atomist is then constrained to acknowledge that his supposed ultimate simples, namely, bare particulars and properties, are not really simple after all.

Nevertheless, before discussing and defending both an alternative solution to the problem of grounding sameness and difference and an alternative analysis of simple atomic propositions, we must first explain in more detail the ontology of contemporary logical atomists, showing (a) how and on what basis they distinguish existence from subsistence, and (b) why they hold that in addition to bare particulars and properties facts contain three formal constituents which cannot "exist" but which must subsist. Moreover, as a prelude to this discussion we shall briefly trace the origin of the naming criterion to Russell's logical atomism papers and to his later work *An Inquiry into Meaning and Truth* where, we shall find, Lord Russell retained a form of the naming criterion in spite of his rejection of logical atomism.

III. Logical Atomism and the Naming Criterion for Existence

As is commonly known, in his logical atomist period Russell held (a) that the meaning of a name is identifiable with its referent, (b) that naming an object presupposes acquaintance with that object, so that one cannot properly name anything with which he is not acquainted, and (c) that only simples are nameable. Since, as was pointed out earlier, (b) is so patently inconsistent with logical atomism, we can only assume that Russell attached a broader meaning to the word 'acquaintance' than that which it ordinarily has. For in his "Philosophy of Logical Atomism" Russell tells us that simple particulars are named by logically proper names. But on the assumption of logical atomism these simple particulars must be bare particulars. Hence, Russell once held that we are in some sense acquainted with bare patriculars, a view which he later abandoned.

But at a still earlier stage in his philosophical development Russell held that while acquaintance with an object is a necessary condition for its being named, nevertheless, the objects of acquaintance which are presented to us in sense perception are always complex entities or facts. We are acquainted, in other words, with what he calls "instances of universals" or particulars and not with universals nor for that matter, with bare particulars either. This is evident from the following statement from "On The Relation of Universals and Particulars" in which Russell presupposes a kind of direct correspondence between the realm of acquaintance and the real realm.

> Thus the fact that it is logically possible for precisely similar things to co-exist in two different places, but that things in different places at the same time cannot be numerically identical, forces us to admit that it is particulars, i.e., *instances* of universals, that exist in places and not universals themselves.[1]

Russell here presupposes an inference from the perception of similar things in different places to the real existence of these things *in rerum natura*. In other words, he presupposes that there is a kind of similarity or correspondence between the independent, self-subsistent way in which objects are presented in sense perception and the self-subsistent way in which they really exist. Nor are these "instances of universals" or particulars, which Russell here refers to, the bare particulars of his logical atomist period. Rather, they are particulars in the sense that "This white patch" is a particular. This is evidenced by the fact that these particulars have qualities or characteristics. As Russell puts it later in the same essay:

> They (particulars) may or may not have intrinsic differences—of shape, or size, or brightness, or any other quality—but whether they have or not they are two, and it is obviously logically possible that they should have no intrinsic differences whatever.[2]

Nevertheless, as soon as Russell began to develop his theory of logical atomism, as soon, in other words, as he began to construe atomic propositions as pictures or maps for facts, he was compelled, in effect, to abandon the notion that we are acquainted with complex entities only. The reason for this was that with his picture theory and the logical atomism which necessarily followed from it, Russell introduced into his ontology such simple dependent existents as bare particulars and universals, neither one of which, of course, could be counted as independent in the sense of being able to exist alone, i.e. unaccompanied by one another. Thus, while denying existence to universals and taking the line that only "instances of universals" exist in his very early essay "On The Relation of Universals and Particulars," Russell in this later essay is compelled, as a result of introducing his picture theory of propositions, to alter his earlier ontological views in such a way that he admitted only two kinds of simple entities, namely, universals and bare particulars. Thus, moving to an extreme Realistic position in his later essay, "The Philosophy of Logical Atomism," Russell adopts what contemporary atomists call the naming criterion for existence.

And yet, in abandoning his earlier "fact ontology" and in introducing the naming criterion for existence Russell did not intend to give up the view that what exists is, or can be, an object of acquaintance. Instead, what he did was to broaden his earlier notion of acquaintance so as now to count as objects of acquaintance not only entities that exist *independently* in sense perception (facts) but also (as the neo-atomist would put it) those that exist *dependently* in sense perception (bare particulars and universals). But in stating in his "The Philosophy of Logical Atomism" that we can name *only* what we are acquainted with, Russell does not mean to say that we can name *any* object of acquaintance. Otherwise, atomic facts, which are genuine objects of acquaintance, could be named, and Russell denied that facts can be named. Rather, his claim in that essay is that acquaintance with an object is a necessary, but not itself a sufficient condition for that object's being named.

Nevertheless, as we have said, Russell eventually abandoned this extended and rather suspect use of the term 'acquaintance.' Suspecting a violation of a basic empiricism in his subject-predicate or individual-character analysis of simple atomic propositions, Russell in his later work, *An Inquiry into Meaning and Truth*, decided to give up his picture theory of propositions, a theory which compelled him to posit such totally unrecognizable entities as bare particulars. Referring to this abandonment of the picture theory by Russell, E. B. Allaire cites the following passage from the *Inquiry:*

> One is tempted to regard "This is red" as a subject-predicate proposition; but if one does so, one finds that "This" becomes a substance, an unknowable something in which predicates inhere. . . .[3]

Commenting on this passage, Allaire remarks:

> Though awkwardly expressed, Russell's point is clear: The individual-character analysis is at odds with the empirical tradition. That is, if one claims that 'This is red' is a subject-predicate proposition *in the sense that 'This' and 'red' refer to unanalyzable entities of different ontological kinds*, then one has violated the Principle of Acquaintance (PA), a basic tenet of empiricism . . . the heart of Russell's point is thus that the individuals of the individual-character analysis are unknowable in the sense that one is not directly acquainted with them.[4]

Yet, in abandoning logical atomism, Russell did not revert to his earlier ontological view that only instances of universals existed. Rather, as we shall see below, he adopted the view in the *Inquiry* that only universals could be counted as existents. For example, in this later work Russell no longer analyses a simple atomic proposition such as "This is white" in such a way that the elements of the proposition, 'This' and 'white,' name two different kinds of simple entities in the world.

Rather, at this late stage in his philosophical development Russell held that a sentence like "This is white" is not a subject-predicate proposition at all, for it is wholly synonomous with the sentence "Whiteness is here." Roderick Chisholm, in an essay entitled "Russell and the Foundations of Empirical Knowledge," describes Russell's position in the *Inquiry* in this way:

> According to this view, we are confronted, in a perceptual situation, by the universal itself and not by a mere instance of it. Thus Russell writes in the *Inquiry:* "We are supposing that there are only qualities. Since a given shade of color can exist at different dates, it can precede itself . . ." (p. 126). He then suggests that the basic proposition 'This is red' is not a subject-predicate proposition, but is of the form 'redness is here'; that 'red' is a name, not a predicate" (p. 120). According to Russell's theory, sense-datum terms are proper names denoting repeatable universals. An alternative formulation is "I-now are redness," provided the "I-now" is understood as synonymous with "here" and not as synonymous with "Otto," "Carl," or "Rudof." We may say "There is something which is redness and is here," or, in other words, "(x) $(x = $ redness. x is here-now)".[5]

It is to be observed that Russell takes a position here that is in one respect at least directly opposed to that which he took in his early essay. "On the Relations of Universals and Particulars." In this latter paper Russell had argued that only instances of universals, and not universals themselves, really existed. Here in the *Inquiry*, however, Russell expresses the very opposite view. And yet, while giving up logical atomism, Russell retains the naming criterion for existence, except that he now admits only one sort of simple nameable object, namely, a property or universal. And curiously enough, Russell apparently imagined that his claim that universals themselves were direct objects of acquaintance in no way conflicted with that basic empirical outlook that led him to renounce bare particulars.

Finally, though he does not explicitly say as much, it seems that in the *Inquiry* Russell is trying to introduce what we shall call naming criterion II as a synthesis of the naming criterion and the independence criterion. Like the latter, naming criterion II admits as existents only those entities that are presented independently in sense perception, but like the former it admits as existents only simple things. This synthesis, of course, is made possible only by the rejection of two earlier ontological views, the view that bare particulars are ultimate existents and the view that facts are ultimate existents, for facts are neither simple nor can they be named and bare particulars are not presented *independently* in sense perception, a requirement presupposed in naming criterion II.

2. THE CONTEMPORARY ATOMISTS' REJECTION OF RUSSELL'S LATER ONTOLOGY

Returning now to our contemporary logical atomist, we find that he would be forced to reject naming criterion II, first because it involves the doubtful notion that universals are presented *independently* in sense perception. A contemporary atomist would deny this claim. Second, he would reject Russell's position in the *Inquiry* because it removes any grounds for asserting that bare particulars exist. No bare patricular, in other words, is ever presented independently in sense perception. But once having accorded ontological status of a kind to facts, our contemporary atomist, concerned as he is with grounding sameness and difference on the level of facts, requires the existence of bare particulars to account for the numerical diversity of two or more similar facts. In fact, in denying that such particulars exist and in affirming the existence of universals only, Russell has no way, a contemporary atomist would argue, of accounting for numerical difference.

But to hold that bare particulars exist is to abandon naming criterion II, since our atomist holds that bare particulars are *dependent* entities—dependent in the sense that they must always be accompanied by properties. Hence, the atomist repudiates this criterion, adopting instead his own naming criterion according to which, since bare particulars as well as universals are named by the elements of simple atomic propositions, they therefore exist.

And yet, *prima facie* at least, it may not appear necessary that our atomist adopt this naming criterion for existence in order to account for the fact that bare particulars and universals exist. After all, since he holds that these two kinds of simple entities are dependently presented to us in sense perception, would it not be possible for our atomist to hold that, while presentation in sense perception in general is both a necessary and sufficient condition for according ontological status to something, presentation in sense perception in a dependent way is at least a sufficient condition for claiming that something or other has ontological status in the sense that it "exists"? This analysis, it seems, provides ontological status for facts and accounts for the existence of bare particulars without recourse to the naming criterion at all.

Nevertheless, however plausible it may at first sight appear, this alternative is not at all open to the neo-atomist. For if being presented dependently in sense perception were a sufficient condition for knowing that a certain object existed in the sense of being a thing, then since the exemplification-nexus as well as the "properties" of individuality and universality are also presented dependently, it would follow that they too exist *as things*. But according to our atomist, not one of these latter three entities can be said to "exist" (i.e. be a thing) without futility. As Bergmann himself puts it:

> Signs are labels (though not mere labels) representing (sim-

ple) "things." Individuality, universality, and exemplification, the three "formal" or "logical" constituents of facts, cannot except at the price of futility, be so represented.[6]

What Bergmann is in effect saying here is that since the three entities in question cannot "exist" without futility, they cannot be named or labelled. Consequently, contemporary atomists cannot hold that presentation of an object in a dependent way is a sufficient condition for according existence to them.

3. EXISTENCE, SUBSISTENCE AND BRADLEY'S PARADOX OF RELATIONS

More specifically, and as regards the kind of futility that would result from holding that the exemplification-nexus, for example, exists, we find our atomist denying existence to this nexus in order to avoid the well-known Bradley paradox with respect to relation. To illustrate this paradox, suppose 'a' stands for a certain individual, 'G' stands for the property green and 'E' stands for the exemplification-nexus that obtains between this individual and the property green. If the exemplification-nexus signified by 'E' were an existent along with the existents signified by 'a' and 'G,' then two additional ties, call them 'R_1' and 'R_2' would be required to connect 'a' with 'E' and 'G' with 'E' respectively. But now two further ties, 'R_3' and 'R_4' are required to connect 'a' with 'R_1' and 'G' with 'R_2' and so on to an infinite regress. Accordingly, it is futile, according to Bergmann, to hold that the exemplification-nexus is an existent (a thing) along with the terms of that nexus, i.e. bare particulars and universals. Hence, contemporary atomists like Bergmann insist that, to avoid Bradley's paradox, we must deny that the exemplification-nexus "exists." Yet, since the exemplification-nexus is presented to us in sense perception, it must have some sort of ontological status. Hence, it is said to subsist.[7]

Pointing to the atomists' need to draw a distinction between existence and subsistence at this point, Reinhardt Grossmann, for instance, remarks:

> The realist, though for entirely different reasons, must make the same distinction, (i.e. between existence and subsistence). To understand why this is so, consider a visual field containing two spots as before, but assume that only one of the two is red, while the other is green. The realist can of course account for there being two spots; and he can also account for there being two properties. But he cannot as yet account for the fact that neither individual is both red and green. Somehow he must find the right individual together with the right property. Moreover, his finding them together must be grounded in what he sees, that is, in what is presented to him in the visual field. Consequently, the realist claims that he is not merely presented with two individuals and two properties, unconnected as it were, but also with this individual *exemplifying* red and that individual *exemplifying* green. In short, he asserts that he is also presented with the nexus of exemplification. *This nexus, though, is not named. Or, rather, any attempt to name it is futile.* Hence, it follows upon the naming-criterion that the nexus of exemplification is not an existent. Yet, the realist will admit that he is presented with it. This leads him to say that the nexus of exemplification subsists.[8]

What in effect and explicitly Grossman is saying here is that, though we are acquainted with the exemplification-tie in the sense that it is presented *dependently* in sense perception, when we are acquainted with the whole complex of a certain individual's exemplifying a property, yet, at the price of succumbing to Bradley's paradox of relations, this relation cannot be said to be a thing. What Grossman's comment also and implicitly means is that while we are acquainted with simple atomic facts, yet these facts (which, as facts, consist essentially in a tying of individuals with properties) cannot without futility be named. In other words, as was intimated previously, if the "existence" of the exemplification-nexus be denied, and if, as our atomist asserts, the distinguishing mark of a single atomic fact is precisely this very exemplification relation, then it must follow that from our atomist's point of view facts do not "exist" either.

And yet, just why is it, we may ask, that the "existence" of the exemplification-tie would give rise to the Bradley paradox whereas the *subsistence* of that same tie would not? Apparently, "existent" entities need a tie to connect them to what they are tied to, while some subsistent entities at least (i.e. fundamental ties) need no further tie to connect them to what they are tied to. As Bergmann himself comments:

> Simples, to form a complex must be connected by fundamental ties. (A class of simples is not a complex.) A fundamental tie needs no further tie to tie it to what it ties. (Otherwise we would be faced with an infinite regress a la Bradley.) In this sense things are and fundamental ties are not *independent$_2$*. That is another ontological difference between things and fundamental ties.[9]

Nevertheless, in the light of this comment, a further question comes to the fore, namely, why is it that "existent" entities do, while subsistent entities do not, need a tie to tie them to what they are tied to? The key to the answer to this question, I think, is found in Bergmann's use of the term 'independent' in the latter part of the above passage. Concretely, simples are, and fundamental ties are not, independent$_2$ because the former do, while the latter do not, exist in themselves.[10] Like secondary substances in Aristotelian metaphysics, the existence of fundamental ties *depends* on the existence of things that *exist in themselves*. Hence, they subsist, which is to say that they do *not* in and of themselves "exist."

In other words, Bergmann does not mark off "existents" from subsistents by the simple-complex dichotomy. To be sure, "existents" are simple, but this does not mean that subsistents are complex. The "properties" of individuality and universality as well as the exemplification-tie cannot in any genuine sense be called complex. In fact, Bergmann himself insists that the simple-complex dichotomy makes no sense at all among subsistents.[11] Hence, some dichotomy other than the simple-complex dichotomy must mark off "existents" from subsistents. This dichotomy, according to Bergmann, is that between being independent (existing in itself) and being dependent (not existing in itself). This is obvious from the contrast Bergmann makes, based on this independent-dependent dichotomy, between fundamental ties and "properties" (which are subsistents) on the one hand, and simple things ("existents") on the other.[12]

4. THE ATOMISTS' JUSTIFICATION OF HIS ADOPTION OF THE NAMING CRITERION

Returning now to the reasons that compel our atomist to adopt the naming criterion, we find that his denial that facts "exist" (i.e. are things) rules out a final possibility of providing ontological status for facts while simultaneously accounting for the existence of bare particulars. This possibility would assert that being presented independently in sense perception on the one hand and being named on the other were each of them sufficient, but not necessary, criteria for existence. Having abandoned logical atomism in large part because it involved a commitment to totally unrecognizable entities like bare particulars, Russell, as we have seen, could not embrace this possibility. However, since contemporary atomists *do* list bare particulars as objects of acquaintance (albeit *dependent* acquaintance) they must and do reject this final possibility for another reason. That reason, of course, is that according to this alternative facts would "exist". But facts are complex entities and our atomist admits as "existents" (things) only simple entities. Therefore, the atomist cannot accept this final possibility.

In view of all the above considerations, therefore, it should be clear that the latter-day atomists are compelled to adopt their naming criterion as a sufficient and necessary criterion for existence. Moreover, it should be clear that the reasons for their adoption of this criterion are ultimately based on ontological rather than on logical considerations. In other words, it is not, in the long run, his atomistic analysis of simple atomic propositions that leads our atomist to embrace the naming criterion; it is rather his attempt to ground sameness and diversity among facts in simple entities of different kinds (bare particulars and universals) that both moves him to adopt his naming criterion and justifies his atomistic analysis of simple atomic propositions. Accepting the thesis that whatever is presented has ontological status Bergmann, for instance, must admit, as he does, that facts have ontological status. Confronted, then, with the fact of sameness and numerical difference on the level of facts, Bergmann grounds the sameness and numerical difference of two or more facts in universals and bare particulars respectively, which, since they are also somehow presented, have ontological status. But since these latter simple entities provide the ontological ground for sameness and numerical difference, they must have ontological status in the sense of being things. But, if bare particulars and universals "exist," that which ties them together, the exemplification-nexus, cannot without the futility of infinite regress, be said to "exist" as well. And since this nexus is likewise presented in sense perception, it must have some kind of ontological status. Hence, our atomist concludes that it subsists or that it exists dependently[1]. Thus, in order to account for the "existence" of bare particulars and universals and at the same time avoid

Bradley's 'paradox' as regards relations, a contemporary atomist like Bergmann must adopt what he calls the naming criterion as a necessary and sufficient criterion for "existence"
(thinghood) and deny that the exemplification-nexus can be
named.

Now it is clear that, once having adopted the naming criterion as a necessary and sufficient condition for existence for
the reasons given, our atomist is forced to reject facts as "existents" for another reason. Holding as he does that the meaning of a name is identical with its referent, the atomist cannot
admit that propositions are names for facts without either introducing "false facts" into the world or else being committed
to the absurdity that a simple atomic proposition means something different depending on whether it is true or false.

The notion that facts cannot be named finds its root in Russell's (and originally Wittgenstein's) observation that propositions are not names for facts. Russell had argued that, since
there are two relations that any atomic proposition may bear
to an atomic fact, (i.e. "being true" to the fact and "being
false" to the fact), propositions cannot be names for facts, for
by their very nature names bear but one relation to the thing
named.[13] Moreover, a name ceases to be a name and is reduced
to a meaningless noise if it lacks a referent, but a proposition
remains a proposition and meaningful even if it fails to be
about something. The only way in which propositions could
conceivably be said to be names for facts is by admitting "false
facts" as existent entities. By allowing "false facts" propositions then turn out to bear but one relation, the naming relation, to atomic facts; true propositions name true facts and
false propositions name "false facts." But at this point and like
Russell before him, a contemporary atomist would repudiate
"false facts" by appealing to what the former called "a robust
sense of reality."

And yet, suppose that, by way of defending the thesis that

facts can be named and hence "exist," one should take the line that, while false atomic propositions do not name "false facts" or for that matter anything else, true propositions *do* name facts. Accordingly, whereas the meaning of any true atomic proposition would be identified with the corresponding atomic fact, the meaning of any false atomic proposition would not, of course, be identified with any corresponding "false fact." However, unless he opts for the meaninglessness of false atomic propositions, the proponent of this view must accept the unwelcome consequence that any atomic proposition has a different meaning depending on whether it is true or false. In fact, as Herbert Hochberg points out,[14] this consequence comes about even if one takes the position, absurd as it is, that true atomic propositions name true facts while false atomic propositions name "false facts," for in that case too, the meaning of any given atomic proposition would be something different depending on whether it were true or false.

The only way of avoiding this consequence is to invoke a Fregean distinction between the meaning and the referent of a name while asserting that only true atomic propositions are names. By this distinction, one can give up "false facts" and maintain that only true propositions have a referent without succumbing to the absurdity that atomic propositions mean something different depending on whether they are true or false. As Hochberg observes:

> Be that as it may, for such a fact ontologist two alternatives present themselves. He may hold that all independent sentences refer. True ones refer to facts and false ones to, perhaps, "false facts." But if he holds that the referent is the meaning of an independent sentence then he is forced to hold that a sentence means different things depending on whether it is true or false. This is unpalatable. Hence, he may separate the meaning from the referent of an independent sentence. He then no longer needs false facts, and may

hold that only true independent sentences refer. Thus he is
forced to the second alternative. Upon it a true independent
sentence would have a meaning and a referent, a false one
only a meaning. The meaning of a sentence would be the
same whether a sentence was true or false. Thus a fact ontology would be "complex" in that each true independent
sentence would, a la Frege, involve *two entities*—a sense and
a referent—or, perhaps, a *complex* entity. In any case making
independent sentences the key to ontological commitment
abandons an ontology of "simples" in the sense in which
particulars (i.e. bare particulars) are simples. For, one may
hold that proper names mean what they refer to, whereas,
as we have seen, a fact ontologist is forced to abandon the
identification of meaning and referent.[15]

Nevertheless, even though any so-called "fact ontologist"
may, by denying the identity of meaning with reference as
regards names, avoid the dilemma of either positing "false
facts" or accepting the absurdity that atomic propositions
mean something different depending on whether they are true
or false, still, he must, according to our atomist, somehow account for the sameness and numerical diversity of two or more
similar facts. But since he goes by the independence criterion,
a fact ontologist cannot appeal, as the atomist can, to bare particulars and universals to provide the ontological *ground* for
the sameness and numerical difference of two or more similar
atomic facts. In short, he has no way of resolving the problem
of the One and the Many, even though he can, by distinguishing meaning from referent in a name, avoid the dilemma referred to above. Consequently, either (1) the fact ontologist
avoids the dilemma by making the distinction in question (in
which case he fails to solve the problem of sameness and numerical difference on the level of facts), or else (2) he must
(if he is to avoid the dilemma above) deny that the relation
between true atomic propositions and atomic facts is one of

naming. But since the fact ontologist makes independent sentences "the key to ontological commitment," he has no way, according to the atomist, of providing an ontological explanation of sameness and numerical difference.

As was pointed out earlier,[16] the contemporary nominalist logician W. V. Quine takes the first alternative. That is to say, by distinguishing meaning from referent in a name he can hold that while true independent atomic sentences name facts, false independent sentences are not names at all. In this way, he can avoid both a commitment to "false facts" and the inadmissable conclusion that an independent sentence means something different depending on whether it's true or false. Moreover, by making independent sentences "the key to ontological commitment," Quine avoids positing such strange entities as bare particulars and universals, for to repeat, independent sentences name independent facts which are genuine objects of acquaintance. And as regards the supposed problem of accounting for sameness and numerical difference, Quine is perfectly content to pass it off as a pseudo-problem since a solution to it can be had only by positing certain occult entities which can never be empirically verified, namely, bare particulars and universals.

However, as was also alluded to previously, it seems that the problem of explaining sameness and numerical difference cannot be either ignored or dismissed as being a pseudo-problem just because a *particular* solution to that problem involves a commitment to objects which, while they exist, fail to be any kind or sort of object at all. The present-day atomist is quite justified in seeking to explain metaphysically exact sameness and numerical diversity among facts; in fact, it would seem incumbent on any pluralistic metaphysics to seek such an explanation. The only question is *how*, not whether, this ontological problem is to be resolved.

5. A NOMINALIST REJOINDER

Nonetheless, in all fairness to Quine, it must be pointed out that he fully realizes that one cannot adhere to both the picture theory of propositions and to Russell's Theory of Definite Descriptions, without accepting bare particulars. More specifically, Quine clearly sees as the following passage indicates, that by a strict application of the Theory of Descriptions, *all* names that occur in the subject-place of propositions can be converted to descriptions which then would be relegated to the predicate or function-place of propositions.

> We can very easily involve ourselves in ontological commitments by saying, for example, that *there is something* (bound variable) which red houses and sunsets have in common; or that *there is something* which is a prime number larger than a million. But this is, essentially, the only way we can involve ourselves in ontological commitments: by our use of bound variables. The use of alleged names is no criterion, for we can repudiate their namehood at the drop of a hat unless the assumption of a corresponding entity can be spotted in the things we affirm in terms of bound variables. Names are, in fact, altogether immaterial to the ontological issue, for I have shown in connection with 'Pergasus' and 'pegasize,' that names can be converted to descriptions, and Russell has shown that descriptions can be eliminated. Whatever we say with the help of names can be said in a language which shuns names altogether. To be assumed as an entity is, purely and simply, to be reckoned as the value of a variable.[17]

Now if this same Theory of Descriptions is combined with the picture theory of propositions according to which the S and P terms of independent sentences name atomic entities of different types, then it follows that the *only* candidate for the referent of the S-term is a certain individual thing that is entirely stripped of characteristics, that is to say, a *bare* particular. But unwilling as we have seen, to admit any such unrecognizable entity, Quine is forced to make the following choice: either he accepts Russell's Theory of Descriptions, in which case to avoid Bradley's paradox he must eliminate subject-predicate propositions and hence the picture theory of propositions, or else, he must abandon the Theory of Descriptions, in which case he must find some other way to explain how one can assert that non-beings do not exist without somehow supposing that they do. The choice is not a difficult one for Quine. He decides that it is better to abandon subject-predicate propositions and therefore the picture theory than to admit that in denying existence to non-beings we automatically affirm their existence. Without the Theory of Descriptions Quine holds, one could not say, for instance, "Pegasus is not," without assuming that he somehow exists.

IV. The Failure of Neo-Atomism

1. SOME DIFFICULTIES WITH THE ATOMISTS' EXPLANATION OF SAMENESS AND DIFFERENCE

Having explained in some detail the philosophical background of the contemporary atomist's preference for the so-called "naming" criterion for existence, and specifically, having shown how our atomist's adoption of that criterion ultimately stems from his fully warranted concern to provide an ontological explanation of sameness and numerical difference, we shall now discuss the ontological and logical difficulties that arise out of the atomist's proposed solution to the problem of accounting for sameness and numerical diversity *via* universals and bare particulars respectively.

In this connection we shall argue that our atomist's explanation of sameness and difference on the level of facts only serves to recreate the same problem of grounding sameness and difference on the level of simples, where it is solved by our atomist only at the cost of abandoning the simplicity of bare particulars and properties. In other words, we shall here contend that to the extent that the contemporary atomists ultimate explanation of sameness and difference is incompatible with his atomism his position is self-defeating. Second, we shall argue that in order to explain sameness on the level of his simples, i.e. on the level of bare particulars and properties themselves, our contemporary atomist is forced to introduce what amount to medieval essences. But in that case his explanation of sameness on the level of facts becomes arbitrary. For if he can explain sameness on the level of his simples by recourse to essences then there would be no reason why our atomist could not explain sameness on the level of facts in the same way, that is, by means of essences. Finally, we shall argue that the atomist's grounding of sameness and numerical difference on the level of facts precludes the possibility of predication on that level, that is to say, precludes the possibility of saying *what* some particular thing is.

Especially when viewed against the background of contemporary nominalism, it is easy to understand why contemporary atomists insist on maintaining the exemplification "is" as over and against the "is" of identity or the whole-part "is," the first of which excludes numerical diversity and the second of which excludes either numerical differences or exact sameness.[1] But concerned as he is to ground diversity and non-diversity, it is no wonder that our atomist introduces basic entities like universals and bare particulars to account for sameness and difference respectively, and consequently clings to the exemplification "is."

And yet, though one cannot help being sympathetic to the atomist's central ontological concern to account for diversity and non-diversity, one must at the same time recognize that his proposed solution to the problem of diversity and sameness is fraught with logical and ontological difficulties. For instance, perhaps the main ontological problem to which his alleged solution gives rise is, ironically enough, the reintroduction of the same diversity-sameness problem on another level, namely, on the level of bare particulars and universals themselves.

More specifically, no sooner does our atomist introduce such existents or bare particulars and universals to overcome the diversity-sameness problem on one level, that is, on the level of complex things than he is faced with the very same problem on the level of simple entities. To explain further, our atomist maintains that two perfectly similar red discs, for instance, each "contains" a bare particular. Accordingly, these two bare particulars are, of course, numerically different. Now whatever these bare particulars are, they cannot be said to differ in any *other* respect, for this would presuppose that they intrinsically and in themselves had some quality or attribute by virtue of which they differed. But being by definition entirely characterless entities, bare particulars do not in and of themselves possess any quality or characteristic. Accordingly, any two such entities can differ only numerically.

Nevertheless, that the two bare particulars in question must be in some sense the same is obvious from our atomist's grouping them under the same category, namely that of "bare particular." But what possibly could be the source of their sameness, the common qualities or set of qualities according to which one would classify them together under this heading?

Confronted with a difficulty such as this our atomist must either (1) deny that any two bare particulars have anything in common, in which case he must concede that his classification of two or more things under the heading of "bare particular" is really without foundation, or on the other hand he must (2) affirm that bare particulars do have something in common in which case he must explain how, just in and of itself, a bare particular can then be said to be devoid of qualities or characteristics.

If I am not mistaken, our atomist would opt for the second alternative, asserting that any and every bare particular somehow has or possesses the "property"[2] of individuality, as opposed, say, to the "property" of universality. Indeed, that the atomist does in fact maintain that all bare particulars somehow have or possess the "property" of individuality is presupposed in his grounding the difference between bare particulars and

universals in individuality and universality respectively. As
Bergmann himself remarks:

> What, then, is the ontological ground of the difference?
> (i.e. between bare particulars and universals) I ground it
> in two dependent$_1$ entities, call them *individuality* and
> *universality*.³

Yet, no sooner does the atomist ground the sameness of bare
particulars in the "property" of individuality than he is forced
to explain how bare particulars can then be said to be com-
pletely and intrinsically characterless.

So far as I can see, there are two ways in which a latter-day
atomist might attempt to meet this objection. First, he might
maintain that bare particulars exemplify the "property" of individuality, just as they exemplify ordinary properties like red,
green, etc. In this way, no bare particular *qua* bare particular
would essentially or intrinsically possess the "property" of individuality but would stand over and against that "property"
in the same way in which it stands over and against any descriptive property like red or green. Accordingly, by maintaining that the relation between a bare particular and the
"property" of individuality is one of exemplification, an atomist might hope to preserve the bareness of bare particulars and
at the same time provide a ground for their sameness.

Second, our atomist might hold that while the "is"-relation
in, say, "This is individual" (said of a bare particular) expresses a whole-part relation and hence indicates a closer, more
intimate relation than does the exemplification-"is," nonetheless, the bareness of bare particulars is not thereby sacrificed,
since bare in this context means bare of ordinary or descriptive
properties only. In this way, our atomist might once again provide a ground for grouping certain entities under the category
of bare particular while simultaneously preserving the bareness
of bare particulars.

Unhappily, however, the atomist can accept neither of these alternatives. The first alternative, though it may succeed in preserving the bareness of bare particulars, does so only at the cost of preventing a solution to the *original* problem of providing a ground for sameness among bare particulars *qua* bare particulars. But providing such a ground is made necessary both by our atomist's grouping certain entities under the heading of bare particulars and by his grounding the difference between universals and bare particulars in universality and individuality respectively. The second alternative, while it may succeed both in preserving the bareness of bare particulars and in accounting for their sameness, can do so only at the price of making bare particulars complex, a consequence that militates against the atomist's repeated assertion that his ultimate entities are simple.

Specifically and as regards the first alternative, if the relation between a given bare particular 'a' and the property of individuality were the same kind of relation as that which obtains between that same particular and, say, the property green (i.e. the exemplification-nexus), then no ground for the sameness of bare particulars *qua* bare particulars could ever be provided. To explain, if the "is"-relation in "This is individual" were one of exemplification, then the subject and predicate terms of that sentence would name a bare particular and a property respectively. Moreover, the entities named by the S and P terms would enter into neither a whole-part relation nor a relation of identity, but rather into a relation of one part or constituent to another to form a complex whole (a fact) which the proposition as a whole is said to be of or about.

In other words, if a proposition expresses the exemplification-nexus, then the proposition as a whole cannot be about or true of what the S-term refers to or names, nor conversely, can the S-term name what the sentence as a whole is about or true of. If the former, then propositions could not then be said to be about or true of facts (since the referent of the S-term, a bare particular, is simple). If the latter, then the S-term could not be said to name a bare particular (since it now refers not to a simple but to a complex entity). Thus it is essential to the exemplification-nexus that its terms name simple, unanalysable existents as parts which are externally related to each other and which constitute the whole (a fact) which is intended or signified by the whole simple atomic proposition.

If this be the case, however, then the "is"-relation in "This is individual" and "That is individual" (said of two bare particulars) cannot express the exemplification-"is," or if it does, no account can then be given of the sameness of these bare particulats *qua* bare particulars. And this in turn would mean that (1) our atomist's classification of certain entities under the heading of "bare particulars" is without foundation, and (2) his grounding the difference between bare particulars and universals in individuality and universality respectively is without justification.

To explain further, if the "is"-relation in the above two sentences expressed exemplification, then the subject and predicate terms in each case would name two kinds of simple existents which are related as part to part. But this means that the propositions in question are of or about complex wholes (facts) and not about what the subject-term in each case names, i.e. bare particulars. Concretely, the S-term in "This is individual" and "That is individual" refers to either a simple bare particular or to a complex particular thing (a fact). If the former and the "is"-relation in each case therefore expresses exemplification, then the "property" of individuality provides the ground for the sameness *not* of the two bare particulars themselves, but rather of the two complex entities or facts of which the two bare particulars are constituents. If the latter and the "is"-relation in each case therefore signifies a whole-part relation, then while the "property" of individuality would then ground the sameness of the two bare particulars in question, the "is"-relation would *not* signify the exemplification-"is."

Consequently, the only way in which the "is"-relation in the sentence "This is individual" and "That is individual" can signify the exemplification-"is" is if each sentence is of or about not what the subject term names in each case (a bare particular) but about a complex whole (a fact) of which the referents of the subject and predicate terms are parts or constituents. But if this be the case, then the predicate term in each of the two propositions would not then signify what the referents of each of the subject terms (the two bare particulars) had in common, but rather what two complex entities or *facts* had in common, namely, the "property" of individuality. Accordingly, unless he is prepared (1) to admit that his classification of two or more entities under the category of "bare particular" is without foundation or (2) to abandon his claim that the ground for the difference between bare particulars and universals is located in individuality and universality respectively, our atomist cannot hold that the "is"-relation in a sentence like "This is individual" expresses exemplification.

A second reason for denying that the relation between any bare particular and the "property" of individuality is one of exemplification—one that turns indirectly but ultimately on the Realism-Nominalism issue—centers on the atomists' insistence that individuality and universality cannot, without the futility of an infinite regress, be said to "exist." But if these "properties" do not exist but only subsist, then the relation they bear to bare particulars and universals respectively cannot be one of exemplification since it is of the very nature of that relation or tie that its terms "exist."

Specifically, the infinite regress referred to by Bergmann would arise in the following way. If the "properties" of individuality and universality existed, then, not being bare particulars, they would have to be universals. But now, if individuality and universality be *themselves* universals, they cannot respectively provide a ground for the difference between bare particulars and universals. Therefore, some additional entities must provide this ground. But if these further entities be universals as well, then the problem of grounding the difference between particulars and universals comes up once again, and so on to infinite regress. Therefore, Bergmann concludes that it is futile to hold that these "properties" "exist."[4] But if they do not "exist," then the relation that obtains between a bare particular and individuality or between a universal and universality cannot be one of exemplification.

Hence, assuming as he does that bare particulars and universals are the only existents, and in order (a) to account for the element of *sameness* among bare particulars (or for that matter the element of sameness among universals) and (b) to provide a ground for the *difference* between bare particulars and universals, our atomist must deny that the 'is' in "This is individual" or "This is universal" expresses the "is"-of-exemplification.

Nevertheless, as was indicated earlier, there is another way in which our atomist might try to preserve the bareness of bare particulars and still account for the sameness. By making a distinction between descriptive or material properties like red and green and formal "properties" like individuality and universality, he might maintain that while any bare particular *qua* bare particular is stripped of descriptive properties and for that reason, bare, still in and of itself a bare particular possesses or contains as a subsistent part the formal "property" of individuality.

In fact, that Bergmann, for one, actually takes this alternative is obvious both from his straightforward assertion to the effect that bare particulars *contain* as a constituent the "property" of individuality[5] and from his grounding the difference between bare particulars and universals in individuality and universality respectively. But these could never serve as a ground for that difference if they were *exemplified* by bare particulars and universals. Consequently, they must be related to the latter entities as parts are related to their respective wholes.[6]

Granted that the relation between a bare particular and the "property" of individuality is one of whole to part and precisely *because* it is such a relation, individuality cannot be said to "exist" for two additional reasons. First, if it "existed" and were part of a bare particular, then, since our atomist describes a simple as an existent entity that contains no existents as parts, a bare particular would no longer be a simple entity. Second, if individuality were to "exist," then it would be a universal. But if it were a universal and part of a certain bare particular, then being by nature one, it could not be part of any other bare particular. In short, there would be in this case but one bare particular in the world. Hence, a contemporary atomist like Bergmann must conclude that individuality is a *subsistent* part of any and every bare particular. Further, he must conclude that since they do not in themselves "exist," the "properties" of individuality and universality are neither universal nor particular in nature.

And yet, no sooner does the atomist take this second alternative for preserving the bareness of bare particulars while simultaneously accounting for their sameness—no sooner does he do this—than he is forced to admit that bare particulars are not simple, atomistic entities after all, but complex entities instead. And this because individuality, even though it may not be treated as any ordinary property, must nonetheless bear a closer, more intimate relation to bare particulars than do ordinary properties. He must hold that individuality is essential to the being of a bare particular. But then a bare particular becomes a being with some essence and hence becomes a composite entity.

But if this be the case, then not only is our atomist unable to represent in his ideal language the more intimate tie that the subject-predicate relation expresses in such propositions as "This is individual" and "That is universal," but also and more important, having introduced such intimate ties, he can no longer hold without contradiction that bare particulars are simple. He cannot furnish any ontological ground for the existence of these more intimate connections, (and hence cannot explain sameness on the level of simples), without admitting essences or natures, without, in other words, admitting that bare particulars *do*, after all, have natures. Accordingly, either (1) he denies that bare particulars have natures, in which case he can neither justify grouping certain entities under the heading "bare particular" nor ground the difference between bare particulars and universals in individuality and universality respectively, or (2) he affirms that bare particulars *do* have natures, in which case he must openly contradict two other assertions he makes, namely, that bare particulars *do not* have natures and that they are entirely simple entities.

But while explicitly expressing (1) our atomist simultaneously and explicitly affirms (a) that any and every bare particular contains as a constituent the "property" of individuality and (b) that the difference between bare particulars and universals is grounded, in individuality and universality respectively. But these latter claims presuppose the denial of (1) and the affirmation of (2). In other words our atomist can hold to (a) and (b) only by giving up (1) and accepting (2). Therefore, either he clings to (1) and thereby abandons any ultimate explanation of sameness or else he accepts (2) and contradicts himself. Briefly stated, contemporary atomists cannot at once provide us with a complete explanation of sameness and yet hold that bare particulars are simple. Yet, this is precisely what they try to do.

2. A PREVIEW OF A LATER THEME—INDIVIDUALITY AND UNIVERSALITY AS ESSENCES

Once having explained, in the next chapter, how the traditional Thomistic doctrine of essences might be offered as a solution to the perennial problem of sameness and difference, we shall argue that the relations between a bare particular and individuality and between a universal and universality are nothing more or less than *essential* relations, since, as we shall also find, his so-called "properties" of individuality and universality have the same ontological status and serve the same function as the classical Thomistic essence. And since this is the case, we shall contend that, having once discarded anything like an essence or nature to explain sameness on the level of complex entities or facts, the latter-day atomists are forced by their own pervasive concern with ontology and specifically with the problem of grounding sameness to reintroduce Thomistic essences or natures (in the guise of "properties") in order to account for sameness on the level of their simple entities.

And yet, from the very outset an objection may be raised as to the legitimacy of even asking whether or not the "properties" of individuality and universality are essences. After all, the objection might run, the atomist's question has never been whether or not individuality and universality were natures, but whether there were such natures or essences as "being a man" or "being a table." Accordingly, while a contemporary atomist might admit that the former entities were essences, he would deny that there were essences *other than* these.

Moreover, along somewhat different lines, a second objection might be raised regarding the legitimacy of this same question. This time, however, the question would be considered illegitimate or inappropriate not because a logical atomist would from the start admit that individuality and universality were natures of sorts, but because the question as to whether these "properties" were natures would correspond to such questions as whether "being a substance" or "being an accident" were natures, and not to the question as to whether "being a man" or "being a table" were essences. Accordingly, the objection would conclude, it can be asked whether individuality and universality are natures only if it can also be asked whether "being a substance" or "being an accident" are natures. But it seems that this latter question cannot be asked. Instead of being an essence, "being a substance," for example, is a category to which various entities *belong*. Hence, "being a particular" or particularity, for example, is also a category to which certain entities *belong*.

Nevertheless, such objections as these, I think, are not unanswerable. As regards the first objection, to admit that individuality and universality are natures, even though they be the only natures, is to abandon the notion that bare particulars and properties are ultimate simples—a notion that is at the heart of contemporary atomism.

As regards the second, more serious objection, we would immediately challenge the presupposition on which it rests; namely, that the question as to whether individuality and universality are natures corresponds to the question as to whether "being a stubstance," for example, is a nature.

To explain, since any nature or essence is not a complete being but *part* of a complete being, and further, since "being a substance" or "substantiality" cannot, like "man," "tree," or "white," be said to be part of a complete being, it follows that "being a substance" is not an essence. The fact that "being a substance" is not part of a complete being is made clear by the radical contrast between the statements "This is a substance" and "This is a tree." Unlike the predicate-term in the second sentence, the predicate-term in the first sentence does not at all signify a *part* of the particular composite signified by the

subject-term in each case. Rather the predicate-term in the
first sentence signifies a certain way or mode in which what is
referred to by the subject-term *exists*. In other words, "being
a substance" or "substantiality" does not signify the "what-
ness" of something, but rather the way in which that same
"something" *exists*, i.e. substantially as opposed to accidentally.
In other words, despite all appearances, the statement "This is
a substance" is not a subject-predicate proposition but an existential proposition. And as such its logical form can be made
evident by rewriting it as "This exists independently." Consequently, "being a substance," cannot be an essence.

On the other hand, however, and in striking contrast, the
atomist's "properties" of individuality and universality are
parts or constituents of complete beings or beings that exist independently, namely, bare particulars and universals respectively. And as a result, the "is"-relation is "This is individual"
and "That is individual" (said of a bare particular and a universal respectively) *does* express a whole-part relation. Therefore, the question as to whether or not the atomist's "properties" are natures is an appropriate one and does not at all correspond to the question as to whether or not "being a substance" or "being an accident" are natures.

3. RECAPITULATION AND REINFORCEMENT OF OUR CRITIQUE OF CONTEMPORARY ATOMISM

Hopefully, our criticism of the latter-day logical atomists is now quite clear. Looked upon as an attempt to ground
sameness and difference on the level of facts by grounding
sameness and numerical difference in universals and bare particulars respectively, contemporary atomism succeeds in doing
that only at the cost of resurrecting the problem of explaining
sameness on the level of bare particulars and properties themselves. If, as Bergmann so often insists, bare particulars in and
of themselves lack any attribute, property, or characteristic

of their own, *by what* are they classified under the category of "bare particular"? Further, does not the grounding of the difference between bare particulars and universals in individuality and universality respectively *presuppose* that any and every bare particular somehow has or possesses the "property" of individuality, as any and every universal has or possesses the "property" of universality? The posing of these questions, we have seen, present our atomist with two unacceptable alternatives: either he must hold that bare particulars as such and in themselves possess the property of individuality, in which case he is forced to concede that bare particulars are complex or else he must maintain that the relation between any bare particular and the "property" of individuality is, like that which obtains between a bare particular and any ordinary descriptive property, a relation of exemplification. In this case, however, by the very nature of the exemplification-nexus, the "property" of individuality would not provide a ground for the sameness of two or more bare particulars *qua* bare particulars, but rather of two or more complex entities or facts of which bare particulars are constituents. Furthermore, if the relation were one of exemplification, then our atomist could no longer ground the difference between bare particulars and universals in individuality and universality respectively since his attempt to do so would lead to an infinite regress.

And yet, as if this inconsistency of both affirming and denying the simplicity of bare particulars and properties were not enough to embarrass contemporary atomists, it appears that they are also beset with the further logical difficulty of not being able to predicate one thing or another, or of not being able to say, on the level of complex entities or facts, just *what* anything is. More specifically, since our atomist totally rejects essential relations or natures on the level of complex things or facts, substituting in their stead the "exemplification-tie" together with its terms (bare particulars and universals), it follows that he cannot make any "what-statements" at all on this level. After all, since bare particulars and universals are two entirely distinct kinds of existents, no bare particular can ever be said to *be* a universal, nor can any universal ever be said to be *what* a bare particular is. Accordingly, in uttering a simple atomic proposition like "This is red" the only thing we would be saying is "This bare particular is *related* or *tied* to redness." But this is not actually to *predicate* 'red' of 'This'; or, put a little differently, this is not to say *what* 'This' is. And the reason for this is that in any genuine "what-statement" about some particular thing or other, the predicate must always signify a *part* of the whole particular thing signified by the subject. Nor does it seem that this frustration of predicability on the level of facts is due to anything else than the atomist's absolute denial of "whats" or natures to bare particulars when these latter entities are viewed as constituents of simple atomic facts. Not having in itself any descriptive or ordinary properties, one can hardly describe any bare particular or say *what* it is.[7]

On the other hand, however, and curiously enough, our atomist is not at all plagued by this inability to predicate of bare particulars when these simple existents are viewed not as constituents of facts but just as such and in themselves. In other words, holding as he does that the "properties" of individuality and universality are each of them subsistent parts of bare particulars and universals respectively, the atomist can in principle at least easily make such "what" statements, trivial as they may be, as "This is individual" and "That is universal." But if he can in principle predicate of bare particulars on this lower level of simples, is it not only because he has reintroduced on this level and in the guise of "properties" what he rejected on the level of facts, namely, essences or natures? After all, like essences, the "properties" of universality and individuality are in themselves neither universals nor particulars, and

neither one nor many.[8] Moreover, it would seem that it is precisely because they are neither universal nor particular that
these same "properties" can be predicated of various universals
and bare particulars respectively without precluding either
sameness or numerical difference. For example, in the proposition "This is individual" (said of a bare particular) if the P-
term referred to a universal and were part of what the S-term
signified (as it in fact is), then no account could be given of
the numerical diversity of bare particulars. On the other hand,
if this same predicate referred to a particular and were part of
what is signified by the S-term, then no account of the sameness among bare particulars could be provided. But since the
predicate in the above statement refers to a "property" (an
essence) which, while it accounts for the sameness among bare
particulars is still *not* a property or universal, then this sameness is accounted for *without* precluding the numerical diversity of bare particulars. And finally, like essences, our atomists' "properties" are as such and existentially neither one nor
many. If they were of themselves numerically one they could
not, of course, be multiplied in various bare particulars and
universals; and if they were in and of themselves many, they
could not be one in any one bare particular or universal—in
other words, each bare particular would then contain many
"individualities" as each universal would contain many "uni-
versalities," which is patently absurd.

In sum, the contemporary atomist's inconsistency in denying that bare particulars have natures in the context of his
treatment and analysis of facts, but affirming that bare particulars do have natures in the context of his treatment of the
problem of sameness on the level of simples is transparently
reflected in, and actually responsible for, his inability to predicate some things of bare particulars (ordinary properties) and
his inability to predicate other things of those existents (the
"properties" of individuality and universality). But at the same

time and as has been noted, his own doctrine of what can and
cannot be sensibly said prevents him from even predicating individuality and universality of bare particulars, the only sorts
of things which *in principle* at least *could* be predicated of
bare particulars.

And yet, such an ontological inconsistency and logical im-
passe as we have just described seem to be the inevitable outcome of an ontology which has as basic entities such "existents" as bare particulars and universals. After all, it is precisely
because the atomist of today posits a multitude of bare particulars to account for the numerical diversity of things and a
multitude of universals to account for the different respects in
which things are the same that he faces the same problem of
grounding sameness and numerical difference on the level of
bare particulars and universals themselves. But on this level
the problem can be solved only by appealing to essences.
Moreover, and in connection with the logical issue of predication, it is precisely because he thinks that the subject and
predicate terms of simple atomic propositions name bare particulars and universals respectively that our atomist is prevented from saying *what* some particular thing is. For quite
clearly, and as the atomist himself would agree, no particular
is a universal, the two being irreducible the one to the other.

This same logical critique of logical atomism can be put in
another way. It can be argued that the reason why our atomist
cannot predicate one thing of another or say what any particular thing is is precisely because he has abandoned the traditional view of propositions as instruments of analysis. For to view
propositions as instruments of analysis it must be presupposed
that what the subject-term of a proposition refers to is somehow complex. But for the logical atomist, of course, both the
S and P terms of atomic propositions refer to utterly simple
entities.

To explain, a traditional (and from our viewpoint a correct) view of propositions is that they are human cognitive instruments by means of which we human beings analyze some complex object for the purpose of gaining and expressing more precise knowledge of an object. For example, when we say "Mammals are warm-blooded" what we do conceptually is both to abstract the property of being warm-blooded from the notion of a mammal and then reunite that property to essence of mammality. For we mean to say both that mammals are *warm-blooded* and that mammals *are* warm-blooded. In short, propositions, according to the traditional view, are *both* instruments of analysis whereby a part is abstracted from a given whole *and* instruments of synthesis whereby the part abstracted by conceptual analysis is reunited to that whole in which it exists and from which it is never separated in fact and in reality. And the strongest point in favor of this traditional view of propositions is that only on the basis of this view is it possible to say *what* something is and what something *is*.

Now what any logical atomist does, be he Russell, Wittgenstein, or Bergmann, is to deny this view of propositions. For according to them, the subject terms of simple atomic propositions like "This is red" are never complex wholes but utterly simple particulars. But clearly, unless such subject-terms referred to complex wholes, of which the corresponding predicate terms are parts, propositions can no longer be viewed as cognitive instruments of analysis and synthesis. But if they are not viewed in this way, and if it is only by being construed in this way that propositions can be instruments for knowing and saying what this, that, or the other thing is, then how is it possible for logical atomists to know or say what anything is? Clearly, such a modest accomplishment is not possible for them at all.

We have argued that, in explicitly denying that particulars have natures while implicitly affirming that they do have natures, logical atomism is self-defeating. Ironically enough, when pushed far enough, the very considerations which contemporary atomists think go to support atomism serve only to subvert atomism. For to repeat, if, in order to ground ontologically sameness and numerical difference on the level of facts, one posits bare particulars and properties respectively, then the question of grounding sameness only comes up again with respect to these latter entities. What is the ontological ground of the sameness of properties? To be consistent our atomist must ground sameness and difference on this level as well. And this he does by way of the "properties" of universality and individuality respectively. But since individuality and universality are parts of individuals and properties respectively, individuals and properties turn out to be non-simple, non-atomic entities and not the simple, atomic things they are supposed to be. And so, ironically enough, the new ontologically oriented defense of the metaphysics of logical atomism when consistently pursued harbors the very destruction of logical atomism. Moreover, and to repeat, on the basis of the metaphysics of logical atomism we are prevented from ever saying what anything really is, a consequence which leads directly to a dead-end skepticism as regards our knowing the essences or natures of things.

But now, if these various difficulties logical and ontological alike issue directly from the atomist's ontology of bare particulars and universals, perhaps a different ontology can be proposed on the basis of which sameness and difference can be consistently explained, and on the basis of which we human knowers can say what things are. Or, put differently, can an analysis of simple atomic propositions be offered which, while it involves a commitment to neither bare individuals nor universals, can nonetheless both explain sameness and allow for numerical difference? And second, if there be such an analysis, can it also account for the fact of predication—for the fact that we human beings make so-called 'what" statements about various particular things?

V. Classical Realism
as Alternative
to Logical Atomism

Faced with the questions raised at the conclusion of the last chapter, we might preface our proposed answers by recalling the atomist's reasons for rejecting both the whole-part and identity analyses of the "is"-relation in favor of the so-called exemplification-"is." Then we shall argue that on the basis of the Thomistic theory of essences, the "is"-relation in simple atomic propositions may be interpreted as expressing or intending a real whole-part relation, even though it is in itself a logical relation of identity.[1] Finally, we shall show how this latter analysis of the "is"-relation not only allows for sameness and numerical difference, but also enables us to predicate one thing of another or to say *what* some particular thing really is.

As was previously explained, the contemporary atomist's reasons for rejecting the whole-part and identity analyses of simple atomic propositions in favor of the "exemplification" analysis are fundamentally ontological. Holding as he does that the identity analysis precludes an explanation of the numerical difference of two or more perfectly similar things (facts) and that the whole-part analysis of this same "is"-relation precludes an account of either the sameness or the numerical difference of the two facts in question (depending on whether the predicate term names a particular or a universal), the atomist adopts what he calls the exemplification analysis of the "is"-relation. According to this analysis, the subject and predicate terms of simple atomic propositions name two different kinds of simple entities which serve, respectively, as the ground for sameness and numerical difference on the level of facts.

And yet, in view of the embarrassing ontological and logical consequences of the "exemplification-is," to which we referred in the last chapter, one might wonder whether our atomist's rejection of the whole-part and identity analyses of simple atomic propositions is, after all, really necessary. In fact, no sooner do we reflect a little on the ontological framework in which that double rejection is made than we suspect that, given a quite different ontology than that which posits bare particulars and universals as existents, perhaps the need for repudiating the whole-part or identity analyses would disappear since, in the framework of this alternate ontology, the dilemma which occasioned this repudiation might not even arise.

Concretely, what we shall here contend is that it is ultimately due to his denial of natures or essences that our atomist is forced to reject the whole-part or identity analyses of the "is"-relation, for given his own ontology of bare particulars and universals he cannot, without precluding an account of sameness or numerical difference on the level of facts, interpret the "is"-relation as expressing either a whole-part or an identity relationship. However, we shall argue that, given an ontology which admits Thomistic natures or essences, one need not reject either the whole-part or identity analyses of the 'is' relation precisely because in the framework of this alternate ontology the dilemma which in our atomist's ontology occasioned the repudiation of these analyses does not even arise. But to show this, it is necessary first to understand what might be called the "existential neutrality" of essences. Accordingly it is to this feature of Thomistic essences which we must first turn.

As is perhaps commonly known, classical realists or Thomists maintain that, as regards the knowledge of ordinary physical things, there is a kind of identity between the mind and the object, the knower and the known. More precisely, the concept or idea that one has of a material object is said in some sense to be identical with that object itself. This is not to say, of course, that an idea or concept of something simple and categorically *is* that something. Rather, what this theory states is that the nature or essence of the physical thing in question, say a particular tree, is in a sense one and the same with the nature or essence of the tree in the mind of the knower, even though, quite clearly, the way in which the nature or essence of the tree exists in the real world (physically and particularly) is different from the way in which it exists in the mind (immaterially and universally). And the sense in which the nature existing in a material way is one and the same with the nature existing in a mental way is that sense in which the nature in each case is considered just as such and in itself, quite apart from the particular mode of existence by which it is instantiated in each case.

Now the reason for this identity thesis is to explain what to Thomists is a matter of indisputable fact, namely, that we human beings have knowledge, however inchoate and imprecise, of things-in-themselves.[2] Without such a theory of the identity of concept with object in the sense described, but with a representational theory instead, the *fact* of this knowledge could not be justified or explained. For if the essence of the idea were not one and the same with the essence of the object known in and through the idea, then human knowledge could never be a knowledge of objects themselves, but only a knowledge of those objects *as known*, i.e. only a knowledge of our own ideas. But since we do know objects and not merely our ideas of objects, there must be an essential identity between idea and object. To repeat a celebrated Scholastic maxim, concepts or ideas are not *that which* (id quod) we know, but rather that *through which* (id a quo) we know. Otherwise we could never know things but only our own ideas of things.

However, be that as it may, the point is this: it follows immediately from this epistemological thesis of the identity of the knower and the known that any and all modes of existence are entirely accidental to an essence. Or, put a little differently, since an essence or nature can, because it does, exist either mentally as a universal concept or physically as a concrete object, it follows that, taken in and of itself, or absolutely, it need not exist in any one of these ways. Taken in itself, in other words, an essence is existentially neutral.[3]

Thus, this thesis that *esse* or the act of existence is entirely accidental to any given essence, explicitly expounded by Aquinas,[4] is vital to the central epistemological thesis of classical realism that we human beings know things-in-themselves. If the doctrine of the essential identity of concept with object implies that essences as such do not necessarily exist either particularly or universally, it follows that the denial of this latter theory would result in the denial of the identity thesis also. But to deny the identity thesis is to remove the ground for claiming that we know things-in-themselves. In this way, the theory that any act of existing (esse) is accidental to an essence goes hand in hand with this identity theory of knowledge. To deny the former is to deny the latter, since to deny the former is to deny the essential identity of concept and object.

Yet, it is not only or even primarily out of epistemological considerations that the Thomist or classical realist holds that essences are existentially neutral. Explicitly, besides providing the ground for the identity of concept and object in the sense explained and hence, ultimately speaking, for the possibility of our knowledge of things-in-themselves, the theory that essences are in themselves neither universal nor particular in their mode of existence allows our classical realist to solve, without recourse to either bare particulars or self-subsisting universals, the problem of sameness and numerical diversity. In fact, if I understand Aquinas rightly, it was mainly to solve this ontological problem of The One and the Many that Aquinas insisted on what I have called the existential neutrality of essences, or the view that any mode of existence is accidental to an essence taken as such or in itself.

Moreover, unless I am mistaken, the way in which this classical doctrine of essences is brought to bear upon the sameness-diversity problem is such as to allow for both a whole-part and an identity analysis of the is-relation in simple atomic propositions without precluding an account of either sameness or numerical difference. In other words, we shall contend that in the framework of an ontology of essences, though not, as we have seen, in the framework of an ontology of bare particulars and self-subsisting universals, the "is"-relation in simple atomic propositions may be interpreted as expressing in different respects both a whole-part and an identity relationship without simultaneously precluding either sameness or numerical difference. Refusing to admit such entities as natures or essences, but conscious of the sameness-diversity problem, our contemporary atomist posits bare particulars and self-subsisting universals in an attempt to solve this problem. But having once introduced these entities, he could not, without precluding either sameness or numerical diversity, interpret the "is"-relation in simple atomic propositions as expressing either a whole-part or an identity relation. Consequently, he was forced to fall back on the exemplification-"is." We must now explain 1) how the classical theory of essences can explain sameness and allow for numerical diversity, and 2) how, on the basis of this theory of essences, the "is"-relation in simple atomic propositions may be interpreted as signifying or intending a real whole-part relation while at the same time being in itself a logical relation of identity.

Having emerged from the Realism-Nominalism controversy in the Middle Ages, the Thomistic theory of essences was in large part an attempt to solve the problem of accounting for sameness and numerical difference. Aquinas' rejection of extreme Realism on the one hand and Nominalism on the other is based on the inability of these positions to account for numerical diversity and sameness respectively. More specifically, if the universal "humanity," for instance, existed *in rerum natura*, then, since universals are by nature one, humanity would be one. But as a matter of fact, human nature is multiplied in the world according as individual persons are multiplied. Therefore, the thesis that only universals exist fails to explain numerical diversity within a given species.[5] On the other hand, however, if only particulars existed, i.e. entities which had nothing at all in common with each other, then no account could be given of the obvious sameness among certain individuals, and hence the classification of certain individuals under one and the same heading would be entirely arbitrary.

This line of argument sounds familiar enough. Aquinas rejects each of these extreme ontological positions for the same reasons that Bergmann rejects them. Yet, though they agree in their condemnation of Realistic Monism[6] on the one hand and Nominalism on the other, they propose very different solutions to the problem of sameness and numerical difference. Following Russell in his earlier writings, Bergmann and his school of contemporary atomists hold both that universals or properties are self-subsistent and that bare particulars exist, that is, particulars which have no natures or essences whatsoever. On the other hand, following Aristotle, St. Thomas Aquinas avoids any such things as bare particulars and denies that universals or common features are self-subsistent. Moreover, Aquinas' particulars do indeed have natures or essences, something which, we have seen, is denied by Bergmann and his disciples.

As was mentioned previously, the theory of essences asserts that, inasmuch as a certain essence can, because it does, exist both mentally as a universal concept and physically in a particular thing, it follows that as such and absolutely considered, it exists in neither way. But this very neutrality with respect to existence is exactly the reason why essences can allow for numerical diversity. Not intrinsically or in itself existing as one, there is nothing to prevent an essence or nature from existing as many, while conversely, not just as such existing as many, there is nothing preventing it from existing as one or as a unity either in the mind or in some particular thing. This is not to say that any given essence, taken as such, is the ground, in the sense of the actual *cause*, of numerical diversity within a species. Such a ground is provided by signate or designated matter which comes about when, as a form, a certain nature or essence is received into prime matter.[7] Rather, the point is that this neutrality with respect to individual or universal existence is a *sine qua non* for the multiplication of individuals within the same species.

Furthermore, it is due to this same neutrality as regards these modes of existence that an essence or nature, absolutely considered, can explain the fact that two or more particular things are the same in certain respects. In fact, it explains sameness precisely because it is the *ground* of sameness and as such performs the function that universals perform in contemporary logical atomism. More specifically, considered absolutely and not *qua* existing in some particular man, the essence "humanity," for instance, is one and the same in various particular men. That is to say, the essence "humanity" in Socrates taken *qua* essence (rather than as a part of the existing complex individual, Socrates) is identical with the essence humanity in

Plato taken in the same way. In this sense, then, the essence humanity in Socrates, Plato, or any other man is one and the same.

2. TWO OBJECTIONS ANSWERED

Nevertheless, the objection might be raised that, in claiming that the essence "humanity," for example, is in a sense *one* in Socrates, Plato, or any other man, I have contradicted my earlier claim that, taken just as such, an essence is neither *one* nor many.

However, despite its apparent seriousness, this objection loses its force once we carefully distinguish numerical or material from formal unity. An account of this distinction is found in the following passage from Suarez' *On Formal and Universal Unity*:

> Also, since "unity" means "lack of division" there are as many kinds of divisions; but in things there is a material and a formal, or an entitiative and an essential division; therefore, there is similarly a formal unity besides the material unity. As a result any individual, for example, Peter, is not only one in number, but is also one essentially; and the individual has both unities in reality and not as a result of the operations of the mind; for just as numerical division is lacking on the part of the thing, so also, there is lacking essential division, whether specific or generic; since formal unity is nothing other than essential unity, it follows . . . that there is a formal unity in each individual."[8]

Here, Suarez argues that there are as many types of unity as there are types of division. But since things are divided both in the sense of being diverse individuals in the same species and in the sense of being diverse species in the same genus, it follows that oneness can mean either numerical (material) oneness or essential (formal) oneness. Peter, for example, is one both in the sense that he lacks numerical division and in the sense that he lacks formal or essential division. A man and a lion, however, not only lack numerical oneness but they also lack formal oneness.

But now, in and of itself any given essence is one in the sense that it is not, considered in itself, formally divided. In other words, an essence, taken absolutely has one definition in all the particular things in which it exists. But this definitional oneness is not the same as numerical oneness. The sorts of things which are or can be *numerically* one or many are not essences themselves but composites of essence and existence. In other words, only things or beings can be numerically one or many. But an essence as such is not a thing or being but a principle of a thing or being. Accordingly, in saying that an essence is in itself *one* and the same in all the particulars that share the nature, I have not thereby precluded the *numerical* diversity of essences. For the claim being made here is *not* that an essence is as such or necessarily numerically one[9] but only that it is necessary formally one—i.e. one *in definition*. Thus, though human nature is multiplied in Tom, Dick, and Harry, yet, Tom, Dick and Harry have one and the same definition.

Another objection which may be raised here is that, in holding that essences absolutely considered are neither one nor more than one in number, Aquinas and his followers are openly violating the Law of Excluded Middle. For surely, it will be urged, something must be either one or more than one in number, there being no logical possibility of a third alternative. But if a thesis flies in the face of the unquestionable Law of Excluded Middle then it follows that that thesis must be promptly abandoned.

In answer, we must begin by agreeing wholeheartedly that something must be either one or many in number and that here is no third possibility. But we deny the assumption, tacit in the objection, that an essence as such can be either numerically one or more than one to begin with. The sorts of things which are or can be either numerically one or numerically many are not essences but concrete things which are composed of essence and existence both. Apples and oranges can be either one or many but not the essence of an apple or an orange. In Scholastic terminology, an essence is not a being or a thing, but a principle of a being or a thing. Accordingly, the thesis that essences absolutely considered are neither numerically one nor many does not violate the Law of Excluded Middle, since essences are not the sort of things to which the predicates of numerical oneness or numerical manyness can sensibly apply. It is not a case of violating the Law of Excluded Middle to say that an essence is neither one nor many; rather it is a case of the Law of Excluded Middle simply not arising, since essences, to repeat, are not the sorts of things that *can* be numerically one or many to begin with.

It is most interesting to note in passing that our atomist's "properties" of individuality and universality are one or undivided in the respective "existents" of which they are parts *in the same way* in which the Thomistic absolute essence is one or undivided in the many complete beings or wholes of which *it* is a part. Like an essence, the "property" of individuality, for example, considered as such exists dependently in the sense that its existence is in and through something else (i.e. a bare particular). Further, again like an essence, taken as such individuality is neither positively one nor positively many since it is actually multiplied in many bare particulars and actually one in any given bare particular. Yet, according to Bergmann, individuality is in a sense one and the same in all bare particulars; otherwise, his grouping certain entities under the category of "bare particular" would be groundless and his grounding the difference between bare particulars and universals in individuality and universality would be unwarranted. Hence, an atomist must hold that individuality is one or undivided in many bare particulars in the same way as an absolute essence is one or undivided in many complete beings. This is one of several important respects in which our atomists' "properties" are like Thomistic essences.

3. THE DOCTRINE OF ESSENCES AS MAKING POSSIBLE BOTH A WHOLE-PART AND AN IDENTITY ANALYSIS OF THE 'IS' RELATION IN SUBJECT-PREDICATE PROPOSITIONS

Thus far, we have presented the Thomistic doctrine of essences as a reasonable hypothesis on the basis of which the perennial realism-nominalism issue could be solved and solved without the necessity of either introducing bare particulars or of reifying universals. Taken absolutely, essences or natures provide the ontological ground for the sameness of two or more things and at the same time allow for the numerical diversity of those things. Incidentally and on the epistemological side, we showed that the doctrine of essences also provides the ultimate ground for the classical realist's claim that we know things as they are in themselves since the proximate requirement for this claim, i.e. that there is a kind of identity between concept and object, presupposes that, taken as such, essences exist in neither a particular nor a universal way.[10]

But besides having an ontological and epistemological function, the theory of essences also serves a logical function, for it seems that it is only by means of such a theory that we human beings can predicate one thing of another, or put a little differently, it is only by positing essences or natures that we can say *what* particular things are.

But before showing how and why this is the case and by way of introducing this logical dimension of the doctrine of essences, we shall first discuss (2) above, namely how, on the basis of an ontology of essences, the "is"-relation in simple atomic propositions can without precluding either sameness or numerical difference be construed as signifying a real whole-part relation while being in itself a logical relation of identity.

To recur to the atomist's example of the two perfectly similar red discs, it will be recalled that in the statements "This is red" and "That is red," said truly and respectively of each disc, the "is"-relation could not, according to our atomist, express a whole-part relation. Otherwise, no account, supposedly, could be given of either the numerical difference or the exact sameness of the two discs in question, depending on whether the predicate in each case referred to a universal or to a "perfect particular."

And yet, given an ontology of essences, is this rejection of the whole-part analysis really necessary? In fact, is it not precisely because he denies any such things as natures that the contemporary atomist is compelled to reject the whole-part analysis of the "is"-relation in such simple propositions as "This is red"? Concretely, by holding that the predicate 'red' in each of the two above simple propositions refers to the essence red taken as such or absolutely, it is certainly possible to interpret the "is"-relation in these propositions as intending a whole-part relation without simultaneously precluding the numerical diversity of the two discs. As we have seen, so far from ruling out the possibility of this diversity, essences, unlike universals, actually allow for such diversity, since, not existing as numerically one in themselves, essences can exist as many in various and sundry particular things. Moreover, by maintaining that the referent of the predicate term 'red' is the essence red taken as such, it is likewise possible to accept the whole-part analysis without precluding the exact sameness of the two discs in question. For as we have seen, considered absolutely, any nature or essence is the actual ground for the sameness of two or more things. Taken *qua* essence and not as existing as a part of any one of the red discs or, in other words, taken in the abstract rather than in the concrete, the essence red in one of the discs is one and the same with that in the other red disc. And finally, not existing in itself as a particular, the essence red can be, and actually is, multiplied in many.

On the other hand, if it is his denial of essences that compels the atomist to repudiate the whole-part analysis of the is-relation in simple atomic propositions, is it not also this same denial that in the last analysis accounts for his rejection of the identity analysis of this relation?

More specifically and as will be recalled, our atomist argues against the identity analysis in the following way: if the "is"-relation in "This is red" and "That is red" respectively signifies identity, then since these statements would produce the conclusion "This is that," the numerical diversity of the *two* discs would thereby be precluded.

"Yet, it should be observed that the above conclusion i.e. "This is that" follows from the two premises *only* if it is presupposed that the predicate term in each premise, namely, 'red,' refers to one and the same thing each time. And holding as he does that the predicate 'red' in each case names a real universal, the atomist must, of course, maintain that the predicate 'red' does in fact refer to one and the same thing each time. But does an ontology in which essences are admitted allow for the possibility that, while expressing an identical meaning, the same predicates in different propositions *refer* to *different* things? In other words, does an ontology in which essences are admitted allow for the possibility that, while expressing an identical *sense*, the same predicates in different propositions have a different referent? If so, then within the framework of *that* ontology the unwelcome conclusion "This is that" would not follow from the premises "This is red" and "That is red," even if the "is"-relation in these latter statements did express or intend an identity relationship.

But now, it seems that the ontology of classical realism does in fact allow for this possibility. The reason for this is simply that any essence at all can be taken in two ways: it can be taken absolutely, i.e. just in itself, or it can be considered as actually existing in some particular complex whole. Accordingly, insofar as the predicate 'red' in each of the above simple propositions expresses the essence taken absolutely, it signifies the same sense in each case, namely, the essence red as such. On the other hand, however, insofar as the same predicate 'red' in each proposition refers to some particular existing whole of which red is a part, then it does not refer to the same thing each time, but rather to two similar, but nonetheless numerically different individuals. More specifically, the essence red in this red disc is different from the essence red in that red disc in that they are each of them parts of distinct existing wholes, each of them actualized by two separate acts of existence. Consequently, if the predicate 'red' both expresses the essence red as such, and simultaneously refers to an existing particular whole of which red is a part, then the conclusion "This is that" does not necessarily follow from the statements "This is red" and "That is red" when the is-relation is interpreted as expressing identity.

In view of this distinction between an essence as such and an essence as existing in a particular complex whole, therefore, the ontological foundation is provided for the possibility of the "is"-relation in simple propositions expressing a relation of identity. Within the framework of an ontology of essences, in other words, we can hold that the subject and predicate terms of each of the simple propositions in question refer to one and the same complex existing whole without thereby precluding the numerical diversity of the two discs. Taken in such a way that the predicate 'red' expresses the essence red as such or the sense *red*, each proposition signifies or intends a whole-part relation. The essence red as such is part of this or that particular red thing as it is part of the universal concept red. On the other hand, however, taken in such a way that the predicate 'red' refers to a *certain* existing whole, each of the two propositions (i.e. "This is red" and "That is red") expresses a relation of identity in the sense that the subject term in each proposition refers to the same existent, the same existing whole which is referred to by the predicate term.

Nor can there be any doubt at all that it is this Thomistic theory of essences that allows for the possibility of the "is"-relation's signifying a whole-part relation and at the same time expressing a logical relation of identity. Concretely, it is precisely because an essence or nature can be taken in two ways, i.e. as such and as actually existing that the predicate term in any simple atomic proposition can a) refer to the *same* thing that the subject term refers to, and b) express the same sense each time which is necessarily a *part* of what the subject term refers to, as for instance, the predicate "human" expresses an identical sense be it predicated of Socrates, Plato, or any other particular man.

4. AN OBJECTION ANSWERED

However, at this point an objection might be raised as regards my seemingly ambiguous use of the notion of 'part.' It may be objected that on the one hand I am claiming that any essence just as such has the nature of a part, while on the other hand I am also claiming that any essence *qua* existing in a certain particular complex whole is also a part. But if this be the case, then it would seem that a simple atomic proposition signifies a whole-part relation when the predicate term refers to an essence *qua* existing in a particular whole, i.e. when the 'is' expresses identity, no less than it does when the predicate term refers to the essence just as such, i.e. when the 'is' expresses a whole-part relation. Does this mean that I must reduce an essence taken just as such to an essence *qua* existing in a complex whole or *vice versa*? If so, then depending on which way the reduction runs, I can cling to the whole-part analysis of simple atomic propositions only at the cost of precluding an explanation of either sameness or numerical difference.

Concretely, if, in holding that an essence is a part, I reduce the essence man, for instance, taken absolutely, to the essence man as existing, say, in Peter, then since the essence man in Peter is numerically different from the same essence in James, no account could be given of the sameness of the two beings Peter and James. And conversely, if I reduce the essence man as existing in Peter to the essence man absolutely considered, then since the essence taken in this way is one and the same in all men, my reduction has precluded the possibility of there being *many* men.

Yet, while admitting that an essence taken in either sense has the nature of a part, I can still preserve the distinction between an essence as such and an essence *qua* existing (and therefore account for both sameness and numerical difference) by insisting that an absolute essence is a part *in a different sense* from that in which an essence *qua* existing is a part. Specifically, the essence humanity, for instance, taken as such, is a part of Peter, James, or any man whatsoever, while the essence humanity as existing, say, in Peter, is not part of any man at all, but a part of Peter only. Being a part of no one particular man, the absolute essence man can be one and the same part of all men, while conversely, being the part of a certain particular man and considered precisely as such, the essence man as existing in Peter cannot be a part of any other man. In other words and technically speaking, the whole-part relation in connection with essences may be taken in two senses, depending on whether the essence is taken absolutely or in the concrete. Taken in the former sense or absolutely, an essence is one and the same part in any and every undesignated whole in which it exists; taken in the latter sense, or as existing in a certain particular or designated whole, an essence is particularized and hence is *not* one and the same part in the various wholes in which it exists.

Accordingly, granted an ontology in which essences are admitted, the "is"-relation of simple atomic propositions may be interpreted as intending or signifying both a whole-part relation in the abstract and a whole-part relation in the concrete since the predicate term refers both to an essence taken in the abstract or absolutely, and to an essence in the concrete, or as existing in some designated particular whole. Finally, and once again assuming an ontology of essences, the "is"-relation of simple propositions may be interpreted not as signifying or intending a relation of identity, but as being in itself a (logical) relation of identity in the sense that, taken as referring to a part in the concrete, or to an essence as actually existing, the predicate term of any such proposition refers to the same existing whole that is the referent of the subject term.

5. HOW THE DOCTRINE OF ESSENCES MAKES THE FACT OF PREDICATION POSSIBLE

Having explained how, on the basis of an ontology of essences and without precluding either sameness or numerical difference, the "is"-relation of simple atomic propositions could be interpreted as signifying a whole-part relation while being in itself a relation of identity, we shall at long last turn to the logical function that the theory of essences serves. Concretely, we shall show that it is only within this ontological framework of essences that predication is possible, or put differently, it is only by admitting essences or natures that we human knowers can say *what* something or other really *is*.

In his early treatise, *De Ente et Essentia*, St. Thomas Aquinas shows how his theory of essences bears upon what he took to be the logical problem of predication. This problem of predication may be conveniently and illustratively summarized as follows: if the "man" predicated of Peter were the essence man existing in a universal way, i.e. the *concept* man, then since universality cannot be predicated of particularity, "man" could not be predicated of Peter. On the other hand, if the man predicated of Peter were the essence man existing in a particular way, i.e. as existing in Peter, then, though it could be predicated of Peter, man could not in this case be predicated of any other individual.

In view of this dilemma and by way of avoiding it, Aquinas concludes that the *man* predicated of Peter is the essence man taken just as such, that is to say, the essence man considered apart from two distinct modes of existence, the universal existence that the essence has in the mind as an object of knowledge and the particular existence that the essence enjoys *in rerum natura*.

In other words, it is precisely because any given nature is in itself entirely neutral to particular or universal existence that it can be predicated of particulars. Or, stated differently, it is this very existential neutrality of essences that allows us to say just *what* various particular things are. Indeed, it is only in and through this theory of essences that we can explain what might be called a logical fact—the fact that we all of us make so-called "what" statements about particular things.

It remains only to show how Aquinas' analysis of the function of predicate terms is related to his view of the function of those logical entities in which predicate terms occur, namely, propositions.

According to Aquinas, propositions play a dual role in the process of human knowledge, an analytic role and a synthetic role. For what any subject-predicate proposition consists in is an abstraction on the part of us human knowers of some characteristic or feature which belongs to the complex whole referred to by the subject term and a subsequent reunification or reidentification of that abstracted element with the complex whole from which it was originally abstracted. The former function of a proposition may be said to be its analytic function, while the latter function of a proposition may be said to be its synthetic function.

More specifically, the linguistic fact of a grammatical predicate being distinct from and being set off against its grammatical subject is a sign of an intellectual or cognitive abstraction of a thing from its own "what," be it accidental or essential to the particular thing in question. Through the universal concept "rational," for instance, the essence rationality is abstracted from particularized existence in the proposition "Peter is rational."

Moreover, as abstracted from Peter the essence "being rational" is considered absolutely or just in itself. In other words, it is through this intellectual abstraction of a part from its whole that we human beings come to know that whole more distinctly and thoroughly by concentrating, as it were, on the part just as it is in itself or for its own sake. But precisely insofar as the concept "rational" in the predicate place signifies a "what" or essence in this way, it signifies that nature (i.e. rationality) as predic*able* of, or an abstract part of, this, that, or the other particular man. That is to say, it signifies something that is incomplete and partial, something which is one and the same in all men. Speaking of this abstracting or analytic function in judgement, John of St. Thomas writes:

> It is plain that logical universality, or universality as a second intention, is a relation of reason to many; this can be understood from the definition of the universal as 'one in many and of many.' But this relation of one to many is anterior to the relation of actual predication. Prior to actual predication, the nature is disengaged from the individuals, and capable of being predicated of them, for the potency on account of which it can be predicated necessarily precedes the act of predication. Therefore, prior to actual predication

there is an intelligible feature predicable of many and a relation of one to many by way of potency and aptitude.[11]

But besides expressing a separation of a thing from its own "what" or essence for the sake of a more precise knowledge of the whole being in question, propositions also and primarily express a reunification of that initially abstracted "what" or part with the concrete whole in which it actually exists. After all, in any proposition whatsoever, S is said *to be* P, even though, paradoxically enough, the two terms are, in the sense explained, separated off from each other.[12]

Now it is just because propositions have this analytical and synthetic function in the acquisition of knowledge, in other words, it is just because the function of a proposition for Aquinas is both to discover *what* something is and what something *is*, that the predicate term in any simple proposition must, besides signifying an essence or nature as such, also and simultaneously refer to that same essence as actually *existing* in the particular whole referred to by the subject term. For to the extent that the P-term expresses some essence taken as such (which is necessarily a part of some composite), a proposition has an analytic function. The copula in this case signifies a whole-part relation. And second, to the extent that its P-term refers to the same existent whole to which its S-term refers, a proposition has a synthetic function, the copula in this case signifying identity. To quote from John of St. Thomas once again:

> Furthermore, when the nature is actually predicated, it may happen to be applied to one individual alone, as when I say: "Peter is a man," "Paul is a man"; then the word 'man' is universal and the actual application concerns only one individual, not several. Therefore, the relation to several does not result from a determinate predication.[13]

What this comment means is this: when, in a simple proposition, a nature is actually being predicated of a certain individual, the predicate term does not refer to that essence absolutely considered or as an abstract part of this, that or the other individual, but rather to an individual whole of which the essence in question is a constituent. And taken in this way, the predicate does not refer to something that is related to or which is in *many*, but rather to something that is *one*.

Thus given Aquinas' view that propositions have the dual function of saying *what* something is and of saying *that* something or other is the case, i.e. given the analytic and the synthetic function of propositions respectively, it is easy to see how the "is"-relation for Aquinas must both signify a real whole-part relation while being in itself a relation of identity. A particular predicate term's signifying an absolute essence allows us to say in a proposition *what* particular things are by stripping the object of the predicate term of both a particular and a universal mode of existence. And second, in signifying the same existent whole which is referred to by the subject term, this same predicate term allows us to say *what* particular things are without predicating a part of its whole. Moreover, by expressing this same identity relation, and therefore in signifying an essence as a concrete part, propositions intend existence or tell us *that* something or other actually *exists* as thus and so.

Finally, given the Thomistic view that propositions are instruments of cognitive analysis and synthesis both, it becomes apparent that Aquinas must distinguish what nowadays is called the sense of a predicate term from that same term's referent. For we have seen that the dual function of intellectual analysis and synthesis which according to Aquinas belongs to propositions implies that the "is"-relation in a proposition signifies a real whole-part relation while being in itself a relation of identity. But this in turn implies that the predicate term of a proposition have both a sense and a referent. To the extent that the copula of a proposition signifies a real whole-part relation, it is the sense of a proposition's predicate term which is relevant, this sense being nothing other than some essence considered absolutely. On the other hand, to the extent that the copula of a proposition expresses a relation of identity, it is the referent of a proposition's predicate term which is relevant, that referent being the same complex whole to which the subject term of that proposition refers.

6. BERGMANN'S "PROPERTIES" OF INDIVIDUALITY AND UNIVERSALITY AS ESSENCES IN DISGUISE

Returning to our previous criticism of contemporary atomists, we shall now try to substantiate further the claim that our atomist's "properties" are actually essences or natures in disguise. If this can be shown, then the atomist of today can be accused of holding inconsistently that bare particulars have and do not have natures. Moreover, if, in order to ground sameness in entities of a kind, the contemporary atomist holds that two or more bare particulars share the "property" of individuality, and that two or more properties share the "property" of universality, it follows that his supposedly simple, atomic entities, namely, bare particulars and properties, turn out to be complex. But then it seems that our atomist must either account for sameness and difference and give up his atomism or else reaffirm his atomism in which case he must fail to account in the long run for the facts of sameness and difference. Second, having argued that the latter-day atomists reintroduce natures on the level of simples, I shall go on to contend that, even on the level of complex things or facts, our atomist must fall back upon natures or essences if he is to ground sameness and difference the way he does on that level and at the same time both avoid the Bradleian paradox and avoid reducing logical form of nothing.[14]

Certain similarities between Bergmann's "properties" and

the classical Thomistic essences are strikingly apparent. To begin with, "properties" like essences do not in themselves "exist." As a result of this and again like essences, they are as such neither universals nor particulars. Moreover, by being neither universal nor particular they can, like essences, ground sameness and allow for numerical difference. Concretely, not being universals, the "properties" of universality and individuality can be multiplied in many universals and bare particulars respectively. On the other hand, not being particulars either, these "properties" can provide the ground for sameness among universals and bare particulars respectively, and hence justify our classifying certain entities under one category, that of "universal," and certain other entities under another category, that of "bare particular." Stated differently, the atomist's "properties," like the Thomistic essence, serve the ontological function of explaining sameness and allowing for numerical diversity, except that, while "properties" perform this function on a limited scale (i.e. just on the level of simples), essences accomplish this same function in a general way.

However, concentrating rather more on the ontological status than on the ontological function of Bergmann's "properties," we find that the key to the thesis that individuality and universality amount to essences of different kinds is found in the notions of *dependent* and *subsistent* as Bergmann applies these terms to "properties."

Subsistence, according to Bergmann, is a mode of existence.[15] And since whatever subsists does not exist independently or *in itself*, it exists dependently. Subsistence, in other words, is defined in terms of dependent existence, so that whatever is subsistent is dependent₂ and *vice versa*. Furthermore, by dependent₂ is meant, not existing in and of itself or a kind of 'shared' existence, as for instance, in classical metaphysics an essence is said not to exist in itself, but to exist in and through that complete being in which it inheres and which *does* exist in itself, namely, a substance.

That Bergmann uses the term 'dependent' in this sense (hereafter referred to as dependent$_2$) is obvious from the way in which he tries to avoid the Bradleian paradox in connection with the exemplification nexus.[16] Specifically, this paradox is avoided, he thinks, by refusing to count the exemplification tie as an "existent," i.e. as something that, like bare particulars and universals, exists *in itself*. If the exemplification tie *did* exist in itself or *were* independent$_2$, a further tie would be required to tie it to what it in fact ties. But this is to invite the Bradleian paradox with its devastating infinite regress. Therefore, the exemplification-tie does not "exist;" it has existence in and through something that *does* exist in itself. We shall argue below that, by making the "exemplification-tie" dependent$_2$ in order to avoid the Bradleian paradox, Bergmann has simultaneously made that tie into a kind of essence in the classical Thomistic sense of the term.

According to Bergmann, therefore, something is dependent$_2$ and hence subsistent if its existence is in and through something in which it inheres as a part and which does exist in itself. By this criterion, the "properties" of individuality and universality are clearly dependent$_2$ and hence subsist. As Bergmann himself admits, these "properties" are constituents of things that exist in themselves, namely, bare particulars and universals respectively.[17]

But turning to the Thomistic essence, we find that, like our atomist's "properties," it too is dependent$_2$ and hence subsistent. Not in and of itself existing, any essence is existentially dependent on the whole being of which it is a part. Moreover, that "properties" are dependent in the sense that their existence is in and through those independent$_2$ simples of which they are parts is evident from Bergmann's observation that no simple can remain a simple if it contains any *existents* as parts.

But there is still another sense in which Bergmann's "properties" are similar to the essences of St. Thomas. This similarity is revealed as soon as we consider *another* sense of 'dependent' that Bergmann distinguishes.

Entities that are dependent$_2$ are also dependent$_1$. By dependent$_1$ is meant that if an entity be dependent$_2$ and a constituent of an independent$_2$ entity ("existent"), then it is multiplied according to the multiplication of that independent$_2$ entity.[18] According to this criterion the "properties" of individuality and universality are dependent$_1$; individuality is multiplied according as bare particulars are multiplied and universality is multiplied according as universals are multiplied.

But again like Bergmann's "properties," essences too are multiplied according as the particulars of which they are constituents are multiplied. Considered not as such or absolutely but as part of the particular whole in which it inheres, the essence man is multiplied in Peter, James, John, etc. Hence, essences are likewise dependent$_1$ as well as being dependent$_2$.

These similarities are striking enough, I think, to warrant the conclusion that our atomist's "properties" are really nothing else than resurrected essences or natures. But if this be so, then it seems that the atomist has grounded the more intimate tie between, say, a bare particular and the "property" of individuality in a certain kind of essences and consequently has implicitly admitted what he explicitly denies, namely, that bare particulars have natures and that they are therefore complex.

7. THE ATOMISTS' EXEMPLIFICATION TIE—ANOTHER ESSENCE IN DISGUISE

It remains to be shown that, even on the level of complex entities or facts, the contemporary atomist must introduce essences of natures if he is to solve the realism-nominalism issue on that level in the way he proposes, and if he is to avoid the Bradley difficulty at the same time.

As we have seen, to avoid the Bradleian paradox, and at the same time solve the sameness-diversity problem by positing such "existents" as bare particulars and universals, our atomist had to make the "exemplification-nexus," a dependent$_2$ and therefore a subsistent entity. But making the "exemplification-tie dependent$_2$ is tantamount to saying that, not *in itself* existing, its existence is in and through the existence of something else which is an "existent" whole of which the exemplification tie is itself a constituent. But since bare particulars and universals are the only "existent" entities, it follows that this fundamental tie must be a constituent of either bare particulars or of universals. This means that in any fact, the "exemplification-nexus" or tie must be "built into" either the bare particular or the universal. But anything dependent$_2$ is also dependent$_1$. This means that the exemplification tie must be a constituent of, or "built into," a bare particular, for if it were a part of a universal then, by being dependent$_1$ it would be multiplied according as universals are multiplied. But such of course is not the case, for there are more exemplification-ties than there are universals since one and the same universal can be exemplified by more than one particular, while there is a one-to-one correspondence between the number of exemplification-ties and the number of bare particulars. Hence, the exemplification-tie is "built into" a bare particular as a subsistent part.

And yet, if we combine this notion of the "exemplification-tie" as a subsistent part with the conclusion reached earlier, i.e. that the "exemplification-tie" is in itself and existentially neither one nor many nor singular nor universal, then what does this fundamental tie turn out to be but an *essence* of a certain kind?

Nevertheless, to avoid the unwelcome conclusion that he has made the "exemplification-tie" into a kind of essence, our atomist might at this point attempt to alter his interpretation of dependent₂ in the following way. He might hold that an entity is dependent₂ if, while having its own act of existence, it is nevertheless causally dependent for that existence on another entity which also has its own act of existence. In this way, the atomist might retain the dependent character of the "exemplification-tie" without reducing that tie to a kind of essence.

However, should he reinterpret dependent₂ in this way in order to avoid making the exemplification-tie a nature, our atomist would then have to succumb to the Bradley difficulty which he is so eager to avoid. For, if the "exemplification-tie" had its own act of existence, (i.e. if it existed *in itself*), then a further tie would be required to tie it to what it ties and so on to infinite regress. Consequently, either the atomist must cling to his original interpretation of dependent₂, in which case he avoids the Bradley difficulty only by reducing the "exemplification-tie" to a certain kind of essence, or else, realizing, perhaps, his implicit commitment to natures, he may reinterpret dependent₂ so as to remove that commitment. But in this case he falls prey to the Bradley difficulty. The only other alternative is to reduce the exemplification-tie to "nothing." This, however, he cannot do, since he is committed to the view that logical form, of which the "exemplification-tie" is a part, has some kind of ontological status.

To conclude then, it seems that even on the level of complex things or facts, the contemporary atomist is forced to appeal to what amounts to essences or natures if he is to ground sameness and difference on that level the way in which he does without simultaneously either succumbing to the Bradleian regress or reducing logical form, or at least a part of it, to "nothing." So intent is the contemporary atomist on avoiding the Bradleian paradox, that he fails to realize that his way of avoiding that difficulty only serves to establish a fact which he would and does explicitly deny, namely, the fact that bare particulars *do* have natures after all, and that therefore bare particulars are not simple but complex entities. But this is tantamount to abandoning the metaphysics of logical atomism altogether.

Conclusion

THE FUNDAMENTAL ERROR OF LOGICAL ATOMISM

In Chapter IV we exposed the self-defeating nature of the new defense of logical atomism. We also showed how on the assumption of the metaphysics of logical atomism we human knowers are prevented from ever saying what anything is. In Chapter V we offered an alternative ontology to logical atomism—an ontology on the basis of which sameness and numerical difference could be explained without incurring these untenable consequences of logical atomism. In this final chapter we shall at last unfold the ultimate error of logical atomism, the one error from which logical atomism with all its untenable consequences flows. This we shall find is the error of confusing a principle of a thing with a thing. We shall here argue that this latter error leads to extreme Realism which is at the heart of the metaphysics of logical atomism.

To expose this root error, we must begin by restating the argument for universals which is often used by the contemporary atomist Gustav Bergmann. Bergmann's argument goes as follows: Suppose we have two spots of the same shade of green. The question then arises, "What is the ontological ground for the respect in which the two spots agree?" It is to no avail to ground this agreement in two particular greens, say green$_1$ and green$_2$ which exist respectively in or as a part of each spot. For then the question would only reassert itself as "What is the ontological ground for the respect in which our two particulars, green₁ and green₂ agree? After all green₁ and green₂ themselves share something which, say, red₃ does not. To avoid an infinite regress of particular greens (which would be futile so far as grounding the color similarity of our spots is concerned) we must therefore hold that the exact similarity is grounded in the character or universal greenness which is shared by each spot.

This is the first half of Bergmann's argument. Its purpose is to show that properties *in some sense* exist because exact similarity exists. The second half of his argument is designed to show that properties exist independently rather than dependently, that they are existents (things) rather than subsistents (non-things). To continue his example of the green spots, Bergmann's argument would run as follows: Suppose the universal green existed dependently in one of the spots as its part so that the "is" in "This spot is green" expressed a relation of a whole to its part. In that case, the same property green of which we are speaking could not exist in the other spot. For by definition universals are one and not many. Hence, to account for the fact that there are *two* spots of the same color, one must hold not only that there are universals, but also that universals are not dependent or subsistent entities, but rather independent or existent entities. In short, whereas only universals can account for the *sameness* of two things, only existent (non-subsistent) universals can account for the sameness of *two* things. This concludes the complex and ingenuine dialectic which leads Bergmann to what is traditionally called the position of Extreme Realism. And it is an easy and really necessary step from exaggerated Realism to exemplification. For if in "This is green" and "That is green" (said of our two spots) the "is" cannot for the reasons given be construed as expressing a whole-to-part relation, the only alternative is to say that it expresses the "relation" of exemplification. But right here and with the introduction of the exemplification tie have we not introduced logical atomism? For if no universal is ever a part or constituent of a particular and yet if these same universals are exemplified *by* particulars, it follows that these particulars must be in and of themselves bereft of all characteristics—i.e. it follows that they must be *bare* particulars.

Where, then, does Bergmann's Realism go astray? To answer this question we need only scrutinize the foregoing second half of his argument since it is here that he argues for the reification of properties. Here, Bergmann argues that since properties are universals and universals are by definition one, then properties are one. But then they cannot be multiplied in various and sundry things as so many subsistent parts of those things. Hence, the numerical oneness of properties precludes their being dependent or subsistent entities, i.e. entities which exist in, through and as parts of other entities.

Nevertheless, whereas it goes almost without saying that universals are in a sense one, is it true that properties or universals are *numerically* one as logical atomists like Bergmann repeatedly assume? For it seems to be a matter of brute fact that properties like green, red, being human, etc. are really multiplied in things, just as they appear to be. After all, and to all appearances, the same shade of green *is* multiplied in many peas, and human nature *is* multiplied in all individual men. Now this undeniable multiplication of universals, essences, or properties is perfectly compatible with the equally undeniable oneness of universals so long as this oneness is construed as formal or essential oneness and not as numerical oneness. Universals are both one and many, but the respect in which they are one is not the respect in which they are many. They are formally one taken *per se* or absolutely; but they are numerically many taken *per accidens* or incidentally. In other words, universals or properties are numerically multiplied only as the particular things of which they are constituents are numerically multiplied. But universals can never be numerically many taken *per se*. Rather, it is complex particular things which are *per se* numerically multipliable.

To conclude then, what leads Bergmann as well as other atomists to their exaggerated Realism and, in turn, to their nexus of exemplification and logical atomism respectively is their confusion of properties with things. But they confuse properties with things in the first place because they reduce all oneness to numerical oneness. Or, in other words, they fail to distinguish numerical from formal oneness. Rightly recognizing that universals or properties are one, logical atomists then proceed to falsely identify the oneness or unity of universals with numerical oneness or unity. But this is to transfer to a principle or element of a thing an attribute which belongs only to a thing. One awkward result of this mistaken transference is that the atomist must deny what to all appearences is the case, namely, that properties like a certain shade of green are *not* multiplied in many peas or that human nature is not multiplied in Tom, Dick and Harry.

So far as I can see, this is the atomist's fundamental error, the error from which both his exaggerated Realism and his exemplification nexus immediately ensue. But no sooner do we have exaggerated Realism and the nexus of exemplification which necessarily accompanies it, than we are led straightaway to logical atomism, for to repeat, if universals are exemplified *by* particulars rather than being constituents *of* particulars, those particulars can only be the barest of bare particulars. And so, the point of departure of logical atomism, like that of Platonism, is a commitment to the thesis that universals are things. But this very thesis of exaggerated Realism itself rests on the fallacy of ascribing to a principle or constituent of a thing something which belongs only to a thing, namely, numerical oneness.

Notes

INTRODUCTION

[1]To be sure, there are a few scholars who deny that Wittgenstein's *objects* include properties as well as particulars. For them, then, Wittgenstein's version of logical atomism in his *Tractatus* is not a form of Realism. (See G. E. M. Anscombe, *An Introduction to Wittgenstein's Tractatus* London, 1959.) Among other difficulties, this nominalistic interpretation of Wittgenstein's logical atomism conflicts with Wittgenstein's flat assertion at *Tractatus* 2.03 that objects "fit together like links in a chain." But surely, two simple, self-sufficient particulars could never fit together in this way. The point of the metaphor is that two objects need nothing to tie them together, that they just naturally complement each other. But if two atomic particulars are linked together they do indeed need something to serve as a link.
[2]G. Bergmann, "Realistic Postscript" in *Logic and Reality* (Madison, 1964) p. 307.

CHAPTER I

[1]Henry B. Veatch. *Realism and Nominalism Revisited* (Milwaukee, 1954), p. 1.
[2]A. J. Ayer in his most recent book makes this same point. See A. J. Ayer, *Russell and Moore: The Analytical Heritage* (Cambridge, 1971), p. 54.

[3]G. E. M. Anscombe, *An Introduction to Wittgenstein's Tractatus* (London, 1959), p. 100.

[4]Bertrand Russell, "The Philosophy of Logical Atomism," in *Logic and Knowledge* (ed. R. Marsh), p. 197.

[5]Even though Russell held that particulars were nameable and objects of acquaintance could be named, it cannot be argued that his logical atomism did not involve *bare* particulars. For by its very nature of logical atomism is involved a commitment to bare particulars. As A. J. Ayer puts it:

> The basic thesis of logical atomism is that the world consists of simple particulars, which have only simple qualities, in the sense that any complex qualities which they may have are analysable into simple ones, and which stand in simple relations to one another. It is left open whether the number of these particulars is finite or infinite. Both qualities and relations are external to their subjects, in the sense that no single one of them, and not even any conjunction of them, is essential to the subjects' identity: in principle, it could have a wholly different set of properties and still be the same particular. Nevertheless, it is only through the properties which it happens to have at a given time that any particular is identifiable. (A. J. Ayer, *Russell and Moore: The Analytical Heritage*, p. 54–55.)

Later recognizing the incompatibility of saying both that bare particulars are nameable and that only objects with which we are acquainted are nameable, Russell decided to abandon logical atomism rather than to give up empiricism.

[6]Russell's universals were atomistic whereas Frege's functions were not. In other words, Russell's universals were complete entities in and of themselves quite apart from their relationship to particulars. From this it follows that the relationship between particulars and universals in the early Russell was an extrinsic and not an intrinsic one. In contrast, considered in and of themselves, Frege's functions were incomplete entities, i.e. not *things* in their own right, but rather *ways* in which things were. For Frege, then,

the relationship between arguments (particulars) and functions (universals) was not a relation between one *thing* and another *thing* (i.e. not an extrinsic relation) but a relation between a thing and the way it was (i.e. an intrinsic relation). Hence, however much Frege influenced Russell on other matters, logical atomism was Russell's own contribution.

[7]This principle states that the indefinable terms in any logical system must refer to objects with which we are directly acquainted.

[8]Stated differently, if according to Quine all ordinary proper names can be reconstructed as descriptions, and if, further, such occult entities as bare particulars cannot be admitted as referents of proper names, then from a logical point of view there are no proper names at all, and hence no subject-predicate propositions. (See W. V. Quine, *From A Logical Point of View* (Cambridge, 1961), pp. 12, 167)

[9]Wittgenstein, *Tractatus* 2.0211.

[10]See p. 26.

[11]W. V. Quine, "On What There is," in *From A Logical Point of View* (Cambridge, 1961), p. 10.

[12]St. Thomas Aquinas, *On Being and Essence*, trans. A. Maurer (Toronto, 1949), pp. 39–40.

CHAPTER II

[1]R. Grossmann, "Conceptualism," in *Essays in Ontology* (The Hague, 1963), p. 40.

[2]E. B. Allaire, "Bare Particulars," in *Essays in Ontology* (The Hague, 1963), p. 15.

[3]According to Bergmann, a "perfect particular" as opposed to a "bare particular," is a particular with a nature. But no two "perfect particulars" are the *same*, i.e. 'red'$_1$ is not the same as 'red'$_2$. For a discussion of this distinction and its relevance to the realism-nominalism issue see G. Bergmann, "Synthetic a priori," in *Logic and Reality* (Madison, 1964), pp. 281–82.

[4]R. Grossmann, "Conceptualism," *op. cit.*, p. 41.

[5]This is commonly referred to as the "Principles of Exemplification" in neo-atomist circles.

[6]Bergmann labels this sense of 'independent' 'indeepndent'$_3$. He also distinguishes two other senses of 'independent,' i.e. 'independent'$_1$ and 'independent'$_2$. Something is 'independent'$_1$ if and only if it exists as a substance, i.e. if and only if it exists *in and through itself*. Correspondingly, something is 'dependent'$_1$ if and only if it exists *in and through something else*. Finally, something is independent$_2$ if and only if it needs a tie to tie it to something else, while something is dependent$_2$ if and only if it needs no tie to tie it to something else. For Bergmann and the neo-atomists all and only bare particulars and properties are independent$_1$ and independent$_2$ while all fundamental ties (exemplification, for example) as well as universality and individuality are dependent$_1$ and dependent$_2$ (See Gustav Bergman, "Stenius on the Tractatus" in *Logic and Reality* (Madison 1964) pp. 244–45.

[7]For the neo-atomists a philospher like W. V. Quine is a "fact ontologist" and not a "thing ontologist." For according to Quine, "To be is to be the value of a bound variable." (See W. V. Quine, *From a Logical Point of View* (Cambridge, 1961) p. 00.

[8]E. B. Allaire, "Bare Particulars," *op. cit.*, p. 14.

[9]As Allaire puts it, the Principle of Aquaintance ". . . states that the indefinable terms of any ontological description must refer to entities with which one is directly acquainted." Cf. E. B. Allaire, "Bare Particulars," in *Essays in Ontology* (The Hague, 1963), p. 14, note 2.

[10]R. Grossmann, "Conceptualism," *op. cit.*, p. 42.

[11]For an excellent discussion of the difficulties involved in various whole-part analyses of the "is" relation, see R. Grossmann, "Conceptualism," *op. cit.*, pp. 41–43.

[12]Bergmann always uses double quotes around the word 'exist' to indicate a certain mode of existence, i.e. that independent mode of existence that belongs only to simples. Cf. G. Bergmann, "Generality and Existence," in *Logic and Reality* (Madison, 1964), p. 74.

Simples, the exemplification-tie, and complexes (facts) exist, but only simples "exist." To set off these independent entities (simples) from entities that exist dependently Bergmann refers to the former as "existents" and the latter as "subsistents."

CHAPTER III

[1] Bertrand Russell, "Relations of Universals and Particulars," in *Logic and Knowledge*, ed. March (London, 1956), p. 113.

[2] Ibid., p. 118.

[3] Bertrand Russell, *An Inquiry into Meaning and Truth*, p. 97, quoted by E. B. Allaire in "Bare Particulars," *op. cit.*, p. 14.

[4] E. B. Allaire, "Bare Particulars," *op. cit.*, p. 14.

[5] R. Chisholm, "Russell and the Foundations of Empirical Knowledge," in *The Philosophy of Bertrand Russell*, ed. Schilpp (Evanston, 1963), p. 437.

[6] G. Bergmann, "Ineffability, Ontology, and Method," in *op. cit.*, p. 51.

[7] In a particularly illuminating article in which it is argued that Bradley uses two different arguments against relations, M.S. Gram holds that Bergmann is unsuccessful in preventing the infinite regress by means of his nexus or fundamental tie of exemplification. (See M. S. Gram, "The Reality of Relations," *The New Scholasticism* Vol. XLIV no. 1, pp. 49–68.)

[8] R. Grossmann, "Conceptualism" *op. cit.*, pp. 49–?. (Italics mine)

[9] G. Bergmann, "Stenius on the *Tractatus*" in *op. cit.*, p. 245.

[10] For Bergmann, for something to exist in itself (i.e. for something to be substantial) is for it to be independent$_1$. But if something is independent$_1$ it is also independent$_2$ according to Bergmann, since, if something is a thing then it needs a tie to tie it to another thing. And so for Bergmann something is independent$_2$ *because* it is independent$_1$.

[11] G. Bergmann, "Ontological Alternatives," in *op. cit.*, p. 129. See also G. Bergmann, "Generality and Existence," in *op. cit.*, p. 80.

[12]G. Bergmann, "Stenius on the Tractatus," in *op. cit.*, p. 244–45.

[13]Bertrand Russell, "The Philosophy of Logical Atomism," in *op. cit.*, p. 187.

[14]Herbert Hochberg, "Elementarism and Ontology," in *Essays in Ontology* (The Hague, 1963), p. 27.

[15]H. Hochberg, *Ibid.*, p. 27.

[16]Cf. *supra*, p. 14–17.

[17]W. V. O. Quine, "On What There Is," in *op. cit.*, pp. 12–13.

CHAPTER IV

[1]cf. *supra*, p. 24.

[2]Contemporary atomists use the word 'property' in double quotes to refer to individuality and universality and to these entities only. See G. Bergmann, "Ineffability, Ontology, and Method," in *op. cit.*, p. 48.

[3]G. Bergmann, "Stenius on the *Tractatus*," in *op. cit.*, p. 246.

[4]G. Bergmann, "Stenius on the *Tractatus*," in *op. cit.*, p. 246.

[5]G. Bergmann, "Synthetic *a priori*," in *op. cit.*, p. 276.

[6]Professor Grossmann has reminded me that the nexus between particulars and the category of particularity is one of "belonging to" which is distinct from exemplification but which is neither an identity nor a whole-part relation. Still, if two things "belong to" one category or class rather than to another, there must be something in or about them that warrants our saying that they "belong to" that category and not another; that "something" is the "property" of the universality with respect to universals. And these "properties" are, of course, parts or constituents of bare particulars and universals respectively, at least according to Bergmann.

[7]For this logical criticism of contemporary atomism I am entirely indebted to Prof. Henry Veatch. See especially Veatch's *Two Logics* (Evanston, 1969), Ch. 1.

[8]And yet, as a matter of fact and ironically enough, a contemporary atomist would hold that one cannot sensibly say "This is individual" or "This is universal." That something or other is

individual or universal cannot be *said*, but can only be *shown*, according to him. Bergmann, for example, holds that individuality and universality are shown by the shapes of the symbols in the ideal language. cf. G. Bergmann, "Ineffability, Ontology and Method," in *op. cit.*, p. 49 ff. It follows then that an atomist like Bergmann cannot in any way say *what* anything is.

CHAPTER V

[1] As we shall see below, this "is" of identity is not the same as Russell's "is" of identity. For whereas Russell would hold that the "is" in say, "This is red" is the "is" of predication rather than the "is" of identity, we shall contend that even in this proposition there is a sense in which the "is" is an "is" of identity.

[2] Just as Kant takes the existence of synthetic *a priori* judgements as a matter of fact and then goes on to explain how that fact is possible, so similarly, Aquinas takes knowledge of things-in-themselves as a fact and tries to explain how that fact is possible. Of course, in both cases one might question, and philosophers have, whether the facts which Kant and Aquinas find indisputable are really facts after all. In the case of Aquinas' alleged fact, for example, the skeptic could muster good reasons for doubting that we know things as they are in themselves. He might argue, for instance, that the existence of illusions and hallucinations show that in these cases at least what we are directly acquainted with are not things themselves but our own sense-data. And then he will ask how we know that we are not always directly aware only with our own sense-data. And of course everyone is aware of how Kant's own proposed justification of synthetic *a priori* judgements and how his explanation of the possibility of objective experience led to the conclusion that we human beings never do know things in themselves. However, my purpose here is not to defend Aquinas' epistemological realism, but to show how that realism presupposes a kind of identity between idea and *ideatum* and how that same identity, in turn, presupposes his doctrine that any act of existence of an essence is accidental to that essence. In other words, stated more broadly my purpose is to point out that

Aquinas' realism in epistemology rests on his metaphysical doctrine of essences. As with most other views about knowledge, Aquinas' view that we know things in themselves is fraught with difficulties. Needless to say, I cannot even begin to give anything like an adequate defense of St. Thomas' epistemology here in a work devoted to a problem in ontology.

[3]By the existential neutrality of essences we do not mean that essences are ever found without some mode of existence. Aquinas would never admit that essence and existence are separable, but only that they are distinct. Essences are neutral to existence only in the sense that they do not necessarily exist in one way; they are open to more than one mode of existing and hence existentially neutral in and of themselves.

[4]See St. Thomas Aquinas, *De Ente et Essentia*, Ch. 3.

[5]The reader will at once recognize that this ultra-realistic view that universals exist *in rerum natura* was the view of William of Champeaux (1070–1120). The absurdity of William's thesis was deftly exposed by Abelard (1079–1142) who showed, among other things, that the consequence of positing the universal *man* as an entity in the real world would be to rule out the numerical diversity of individual men. If the universal *man* exists *in rerum natura*, then Socrates, Plato and all other individual men are really one man and not many, which is absurd.

[6]I am using the term 'Realistic Monism' to describe the view, held by Russell in his *An Inquiry into Meaning and Truth*, that only universals exist. (cf. above, p. 45 ff.)

[7]No doubt there are various difficulties with this Thomistic notion of signate matter as the principle of individuation and hence of numerical diversity. Fortunately, though, we need not take up these difficulties since our only purpose here is to show how Aquinas' doctrine of essence allows for the *possibility* of the multiplication of essences or universals, whereas the atomists' account of universals precludes this possibility from the very start.

[8]Suarez, Francis, *On Formal and Universal Unity*, Trans. By J. F. Ross (Milwaukee, 1964) p. 33–34. This same distinction between

numerical (material) and formal unity is made by John of St. Thomas who explicitly attributes formal unity to an essence taken absolutely. (See John of St. Thomas, *The Material Logic of John of St. Thomas* trans. Simon *et al.* (Chicago, 1955), p. 104.

[9]As shall be pointed out in the concluding chapter, the logical atomists' fundamental error is that they confuse formal oneness with numerical oneness. When atomists insist that properties or universals are one, they falsely take 'one' here to mean numerically one (instead of formally one). For this reason they must deny that properties can be multiplied. For this reason too, they must hold that properties are things and not principles of things (or what they call subsistents) since only things can be numerically one or many. Thus the logical atomist's extreme Realism rests on his confusing formal unity with numerical unity.

[10]Once again, my purpose here is not to defend epistemological realism, but to show that such a realistic view of knowledge is possible only on the assumption of a kind of identity between the knower and the known. And St. Thomas' doctrine of essences is one hypothesis (though, to be sure, there may be others) on the basis of which this identity can be explained.

[11]John of St. Thomas, *op. cit.*, p. 128.

[12]For a recent and lucid explanation of the Thomistic view of propositions, including an account of the analytic and synthetic functions of propositions, see Henry B. Veatch, *Intentional Logic* (New Haven, 1952), p. 154–213.

[13]John of St. Thomas, *op. cit.*, p. 128.

[14]Bergmann insists that the exemplification-tie, as well as anything else that belongs to logical form (i.e. the logical connectives, the shapes of signs, etc.) has *some* kind of ontological status. In fact, he criticizes Wittgenstein for reducing logical form in general, and hence the exemplification-tie in particular, to "nothing." See G. Bergmann, "The Glory and Misery of Wittgenstein," in *op. cit.*, p. 230 ff.

[15]G. Bergmann, "Meaning," in *op. cit.*, p. 88.

[16]G. Bergmann, "Stenius on the *Tractatus*," in *op. cit.*, p. 245.

[17]G. Bergmann, "Synthetic a priori," in *op. cit.*, p. 276.

[18]G. Bergmann, "Stenius on the *Tractatus*," in *op. cit.*, pp. 244–45.

Index

Allaire, E. B., 24, 28, 31; on Russell's abandonment of logical atomism, 39, 108
Anscombe, G.E.M., 12
Aristotle, 78
atomism (see logical atomism)
Ayer, A.J., and logical atomism, 106
bare particulars, 6ff., 14, 17, 24–26; their alleged incompatibility with empiricism, 6ff., 24, 26, 27, 29; their original logical derivation, 13, 14; their ontological justification in neo-atomism, 15, 17–18, 24–25; their relation to the Theory of Descriptions and the picture theory of propositions, 16–17; the neo-atomist's embarrassment of both affirming and denying that they have natures and that they are simples, 61ff.; their containing the "property" of individuality, 61–62
Bergmann, Gustav and logical atomism, 1–2, 12, 24, 101; and Realism, 2ff., 101–04; and Empiricism, 5ff.; his distinction between existence and subsistence, 43, 45, 78–79, 94ff.; his use of 'independent' and 'dependent', 26, 95–97; and Bradley's paradox of relations, 43–45
Bradley, F. H., 43, 45, 53, 94, 96, 98, 99
Chisholm, R. M., on Russell's later Realism, 40

dependence (see independence)
Descriptions, Theory of, 16–17, 52–53
empiricism, 6ff., 24, 25, 27, 28–29; in Quine, 16, 19–20
essence (see Thomistic essences)
exemplification: 32ff.; as a formal constituent of facts, 43; and Bradley's paradox, 43–45, 96; as dependent, 108; as an essence, 34–35, 98–99
fact-ontology, 108; and the independence criterion for existence, 26; in Russell, 38; and naming, 49–50
Frege, G. and function-argument schema, 13–14, 18; his Realism contrasted with Russell's, 106; and naming, 49–50
Gram, M. S., 109
Grossman, R., on the distinction between existence and subsistence, 44–45; on the "is" relation, 108
Hochberg, H., and the problem of reference, 49–50
independence vs. dependence in Bergmann, 108; 95ff.
independence criterion vs. naming criterion in neo-atomism, 23ff.
individuality: as a formal constituent of facts, 43; as grounding sameness among bare particulars, 57; as a subsistent entity, 62; as an essence, 80ff., 94ff.
John of St. Thomas, 91–93, 112–113

115